SUCCESS REBEL GO GUIDE

Ali Craig

GIRL WITH DRIVE PRESS

iv

Girl With Drive Press
9221 E Baseline Rd Ste A109-600
Mesa, AZ 85209
www.girlwithdrivepress.com
(347)215.4091

Ordering Information:

Quantity sales. Special discounts are available on quantity purchases by corporations, associations, and others. For details, contact the publisher at the address above. Orders by U.S. trade bookstores and wholesalers.

Printed in the United States of America
PRINT: ISBN—978-1-7322841-2-8

The main category of the book
—Interpersonal Relationships
First Edition
10 9 8 7 6 5 4 3 2 1

Hey Beaut!

In both the *Success Rebel* book and this Guide, you will see references to several businesses and a lot of terms. Many of these businesses are mine—each held under distinct LLCs. Also, you will see a few trademark terms along the way.

Such as:

SOULFIRE ® SUCCESS REBEL™ SOUL TARGET™ NOTORIETY™ ENTREVENTURE® NERI® NEURO HUMAN BRANDING® INTELLIGENT INFLUENCE™ EMPiHER®

These trademarks are held by one of my various LLC entities. Please go to each company's website for all the legal 411 as well as the latest skinny.

Love + Gratitude,

Ali

TABLE OF CONTENTS

NOTE FROM ALI

I am a firm believer that knowledge is great, but action is way better. This *Success Rebel Go Guide* is designed for you to do just that—get going, being, creating, and living the life of NEW NOTORIETY that you have always dreamed of.

Just like with *Success Rebel,* the book, this *Go Guide* is created due to the fact that you are a human being. We are using your biology, social stories, subconscious mind, and personality to your advantage, growth, and success. And just like with the book, I am holding the space for you to fully step into who you are, the success your heart desires, and the life of NEW NOTORIETY you are meant to be living.

My goal is for you to take simple action that creates big results in your life.

So, let's roll.

Love + Gratitude,

Ali Craig

DECLARE YOUR SUCCESS REBEL STATUS

YOU HAVE TO OWN WHO YOU ARE. DECLARE YOUR SUCCESS REBEL STATUS TO YOURSELF AT LEAST TWICE A DAY. READ IT. SIGN IT. DECLARE IT. BE IT.

I believe and declare that I am designed with a unique purpose, aka a SOULFIRE. I am destined for success. I am part of a Divine team. I am not alone.

I know that success comes through service. I take care of myself so I can best serve others. I rebel against the social stories and relationships that have limited me instead of lifted me.

There is a solution to everything. I know that my role as a leader is to intelligently influence the people I am called to serve. I believe that everything in life is about relationships. I know that we have more in common than we have differences.

I know that my intentions rule everything. That consistency is king. It is my duty to show a little more love in everything I do.

I rebel against social programming, pull down the hologram of pain, and step into my heart's desire to truly have the life of NEW NOTORIETY.

I am a Success Rebel.

Your Signature

MY HEART AND MIND
HAVE BROKEN FREE
OF THE SOCIAL TIES
THAT STRANGLE MY
DIVINELY IMPLANTED
SUCCESS.

LEARN.

THE STATUS QUO WON'T GET ME THE SUCCESS MY HEART
DREAMS OF.

DO.

BEGIN TO QUESTION THE MOTIVES BEHIND THE MESSAGES YOU ARE RECEIVING.

BELIEVE.

KNOW WITHOUT A SHADOW OF A DOUBT THAT YOUR RAW,
UNBIASED DREAMS CAN BE YOUR REALITY.

BECOME.

EVALUATE WHAT YOU SAY YOU WANT AND WHO YOU SAY YOU WANT TO BE. BEGIN TO CONSCIOUSLY CHOOSE HOW, WHEN, AND WHERE YOU SHOW UP.

CONNECT.

GOING AGAINST THE SOCIAL NORMS IS DESIGNED TO BE A VERY LONELY AND ISOLATING ROAD, BUT IT DOESN'T HAVE TO BE. USE MEDIA OUTLETS, SOCIAL MEDIA, AND GROUPS TO YOUR ADVANTAGE. GO INTO SITUATIONS TO TEST YOUR SKILLS OF UNCOVERING AND OBSERVING THE SOCIAL BIASES WE ALL HAVE. AND WHEN YOU LOOK FOR A "SAFE SPACE" TO CONNECT WITH LIKE-MINDED SUCCESS REBELS GO TO (HTTP://SUCCESSREBELSOCIETY.COM).

I RECOGNIZE, ON A CELLULAR CHANGING LEVEL, THAT I AM DESIGNED TO HAVE A GREATER IMPACT AND INFLUENCE THAN MY CURRENT LIFE REFLECTS.

LEARN.

No matter what people say, you are fully capable of being, living, and evolving into the person you have always dreamed of being. Check out my Break Free Hack that helps you overcome the social stories that hold you back.

DO.

TAKE TIME OUT OF YOUR BUSY SCHEDULE AND DAYDREAM.
IMAGINE YOURSELF ACHIEVING YOUR DREAMS AND LIVING THE
LIFE OF NEW NOTORIETY YOU HAVE ALWAYS DESIRED.

BELIEVE.

YOUR THOUGHTS ARE MORE POWERFUL THAN YOU HAVE EVER
IMAGINED. RECOGNIZE THIS POWER AND THEN USE IT WISELY.

BECOME.

TAKE AN AUDIT OF EVERYTHING AND EVERYONE YOU EXPOSE YOURSELF TO EVERYDAY. FROM THE MUSIC TO WHICH YOU LISTEN, TO THE SMALL TALK ON THE ELEVATOR, TO THE TV SHOW YOU FALL ASLEEP TO EACH NIGHT. BECOME CONSCIOUSLY AWARE OF THE STORIES, TONES, AND ENERGIES THESE PEOPLE AND THINGS PRODUCE.

CONNECT.

RECONNECT WITH THOSE CHILDHOOD DREAMS. THINK BACK TO YOUR EARLIEST MEMORIES OF WHAT MADE YOU HAPPY AND ASK YOURSELF "WHY?" THEN FIND NEW WAYS TO LIVE THAT "WHY" TODAY.

BREAKING FREE HACK

OVERCOME THE SOCIAL STORIES THAT HOLD YOU BACK. TAKE TIME THROUGHOUT YOUR DAY, WHEN YOU FEEL STRESSED, OVERWHELMED, OR EMOTIONAL, TO ASK YOURSELF THE FOLLOWING QUESTIONS.

What do I feel right now?

_____

_____

_____

_____

_____

_____

Am I feeling love for the work, my co-workers, and the other people around me?

_____

_____

_____

_____

_____

_____

_____

_____

_____

Am I consciously trying to be in service through what I am doing?

_____

_____

_____

_____

_____

_____

_____

_____

_____

_____

What is my intention at this moment?

_____

_____

_____

_____

_____

_____

_____

_____

I HAVE BROKEN FREE OF THE MENTAL STRONGHOLDS THAT WERE UNKNOWINGLY SABOTAGING THE DESIRES OF MY HEART AND MY SUCCESS.

LEARN.

THE STORIES AND EXPECTATIONS THAT HAVE BEEN
INDOCTRINATED INTO US SINCE BIRTH IS SOCIAL INOCULATION
OF MASS MINDSET MENTALITY.

DO.

QUESTION THE WHENS, WHERES, AND WHYS, WHICH DEFINE
YOUR DAILY LIFE.

BELIEVE.

BREAKING FROM A CULT MINDSET STARTS WITH A CRACK. YOU DON'T KNOW EVERYTHING, BUT YOU KNOW YOU KNOW ENOUGH.

BECOME.

Choose to lose the pressure, unfulfillment, mental and emotional beratement of The Others and step into the lighthearted, joy-filled, excitement that is meant to be your success filled life. Welcome to your life of New Notoriety.

CONNECT.

A SUCCESSFUL LIFE IS ABOUT CHOICE AND CONNECTIONS.
BEGIN TO MAKE CONSCIOUS CHOICES ABOUT WHO, WHEN,
AND WHY YOU ARE BUILDING THESE RELATIONSHIPS. IF HARRY
AND MEGHAN CAN BREAK FREE, SO CAN YOU.

1

OWN, IDENTIFY, AND TAKE ACTION ON YOUR POTENTIAL, POSSIBILITIES, PURPOSE, AND POWER

I PURSUE UNBIASEDLY WHAT SPARKS MY SOUL.

LEARN.

THE IDEAS, PEOPLE, AND THINGS WHICH SPARK YOUR SOUL IS
WHAT WILL SPARK YOUR SUCCESS.

DO.

GET CLEAR ON WHAT YOU REALLY WANT. WRITE A LIST OF
EVERYTHING YOU THINK BEING SUCCESSFUL IS. FROM WHAT
YOU OWN, TO WHERE YOU LIVE, WHAT YOU WEAR, TO WHO
YOU HANG OUT WITH, ETC. THEN NEXT TO EACH ITEM ON THE
LIST ASK YOURSELF "WHY." IF YOU HAVE A LOGICAL REASON
AND NO HEART-STIRRING REACTION, IT MAY NOT BE YOUR
VERSION OF SUCCESS AFTER ALL.

BELIEVE.

NEVER FORGET THAT IF YOU STARTED FROM A SPARK, THAT FIRE IS STILL GROWING, BUILDING, AND PRODUCING. YOUR POSSIBILITIES AREN'T OVER UNTIL YOU ARE BACK ON THE OTHER SIDE OF HEAVEN.

BECOME.

STEP INTO THE DIVINE ENERGY THAT IS INSIDE OF YOU. OWN
THE FACT THAT YOU HAVE PURPOSE, VALUE, AND A MESSAGE
THAT PEOPLE NEED TO HEAR. EVEN IF YOU MAY NOT BE ABLE TO
ARTICULATE IT AT THIS MOMENT. IT IS STILL INSIDE OF YOU.

CONNECT.

THE SPARK OF CONCEPTION IS UNSEEN TO MOST EXCEPT THE DIVINE. EVEN AS YOU GROW IN YOUR MOTHER'S WOMB, ONLY THE CREATOR KNOWS ALL OF YOUR IDIOSYNCRASIES AND DEPTHS. CONNECT WITH YOUR HEART AND DIVINITY FIRST BEFORE YOU SHARE YOUR SPARK WITH OTHERS. HEAD ON OVER TO HTTP://SUCCESSREBELSOCIETY.COM TO DOWNLOAD THE AUDIO TRACK OF ME PERSONALLY TEACHING YOU HOW TO DO JUST THAT.

THE SPARK THAT STARTED IN ME HAS TURNED INTO A RAGING FIRE THAT INSPIRES ME.

LEARN.

NO MATTER WHAT THE MEDIA TELLS YOU, HUMAN BEINGS ARE
MORE ALIKE THAN THEY ARE DIFFERENT.

_____

_____

_____

_____

_____

_____

_____

_____

_____

_____

_____

_____

_____

_____

_____

_____

_____

_____

_____

_____

_____

_____

_____

DO.

DELVE DEEPER ON HOW THE HUMAN BODY AND MIND REALLY
WORK.

BELIEVE.

OUR WORDS ARE ONLY ONE PART OF THE LARGER MESSAGE
AND IMPRESSION WE MAKE.

BECOME.

A LIFE OF INFLUENCE, SUCCESS, AND NOTORIETY OCCURS
WHEN YOU MASTER THE VERBAL, NONVERBAL, AND ENERGETIC
COMMUNICATIONS THAT LIE WITHIN YOU.

CONNECT.

ONCE YOU KNOW INTELLECTUALLY WHAT YOU ARE TRULY CAPABLE OF, BEGIN TO TEST THE THEORIES OUT ON YOURSELF. HOW DO YOU FEEL AROUND CERTAIN COLORS? CAN YOU CONTROL HOW FAR YOUR HEART'S ELECTROMAGNETIC FIELD GOES? BEGIN TO CONNECT WITH YOUR BODY TO TAP INTO THE DIVINE POWER THAT LIES WITHIN YOU.

MY ACTIONS, PASSIONS, DRIVES, RELATIONSHIPS, AND MOTIVES ALWAYS SET MY SOUL ON FIRE.

LEARN.

BEING YOUR BEST IS A SERVICE TO THE WORLD NOT FOR YOURSELF.

DO.

TAKE TIME TO MULL OVER WHAT TRULY DEFINES YOUR
SOULFIRE FOR YOU.

BELIEVE.

NEVER FORGET THAT HOW YOU SEE THE WORLD IS A UNIQUE
GIFT GIVEN SOLELY TO YOU.

BECOME.

CLARITY IS DIVINITY. REFINE YOURSELF SO THAT YOU ARE
CLEAR ABOUT WHO YOU ARE WITH YOURSELF AND THE WORLD.

CONNECT.

TAKE TIME TO REALLY UNDERSTAND WHAT YOUR SOULFIRE IS FOR YOU. TAP INTO RESOURCES LIKE SOULFIRE.LIFE AND MY WEEKLY PODCASTS, SOULFIRE LIFE AND SUCCESS REBEL; LEARN TO DISCOVER THE DEPTH OF YOUR DIVINE PURPOSE.

I FULLY RECOGNIZE MY POWER AND PURPOSE THAT IS WITHIN.

LEARN.

THE DESIRES OF YOUR HEART AREN'T A SOLO ACT. THIS IS A
SOUL PARTNERSHIP. THROUGH THIS PERSPECTIVE, YOU CAN
SEE HOW YOUR DREAMS CAN BE A REALITY WHEN YOU
ACKNOWLEDGE YOUR DIVINE PURPOSE AND PARTNER.

DO.

TAKE BACK THE WORDS THAT LIGHT YOU ON FIRE AND STIR YOUR HEART. SOCIAL PERCEPTION OF WORDS DOESN'T MATTER IF THEY STIR YOUR SOUL.

BELIEVE.

YOU ARE FULLY CAPABLE OF HAVING EVERY SINGLE DREAM
COME TO PASS BECAUSE YOU ARE NOT ALONE IN THE
CREATION.

BECOME.

GET CLEAR IN YOUR HEART AND MIND ABOUT WHAT THIS
DIVINE PARTNERSHIP MEANS SO THAT YOU DON'T FALL INTO
SOCIETY'S BELIEF OF SOLO SUCCESS.

CONNECT.

CONNECT WITH THE TRUE BLESSING YOUR SOULFIRE IS. IT IS A DIVINE PARTNERSHIP. A FULFILLMENT TO YOUR SOUL AND YOU ARE BLESSED ENOUGH TO LIVE, WORK, AND BREATHE THE EARTHLY BENEFITS THROUGH LIVING A LIFE OF NEW NOTORIETY.

I WILL FOREVER REALIZE THE UNENDING DEPTH OF BRILLIANCE THAT LIES INSIDE OF ME.

LEARN.

JUST BECAUSE YOU HAVE DENIED THE CALLINGS OF YOUR
HEART, YOUR SOULFIRE, YOUR ENTIRE LIFE UP UNTIL NOW.
YOU STILL HAVE TIME TO TAKE ACTION.

DO.

TAKE CONSCIOUS EFFORT DAILY TO CONNECT WITH OTHERS, STIMULATE YOUR HEART, AND HAVE MEANINGFUL PHYSICAL CONTACT WITH THOSE YOU LOVE AND LOVE YOU. EVEN IF IT IS YOUR FURRY FOUR-LEGGED FAMILY MEMBER.

BELIEVE.

YOU ARE NO ACCIDENT. THE SPARK THAT FORMED YOU IS STILL
THERE. NEVER FORGET THE DIVINE SPARK IS STILL INSIDE OF
YOU.

BECOME.

Rebels are warriors. You must be willing to fight for your heart, the people you are meant to be of service to and for your Divine Partnership.

CONNECT.

THE TRUTH IS: IT IS ALL POSSIBLE. CONNECT WITH THAT. BREATHE THAT AND BELIEVE THAT. UNTIL YOU KNOW IN EVERY OUNCE OF YOUR BEING THAT YOUR SOULFIRE IS POSSIBLE THROUGH YOU AND WITH YOU.

MY MIND IS DIVINELY FOCUSED—SOLELY ON THE DREAMS OF MY HEART.

LEARN.

LOVE IS YOUR NATURAL STATE. WHEN I WORK, SPEAK, OR REACT OUT OF ANYTHING LESS THAN LOVE I AM OUT OF MY DIVINE PARTNERSHIP.

DO.

SET YOUR PHONE ALARM OR REMINDER IN YOUR SCHEDULE FOR
A QUICK "90 SECOND CHECK IN" WITH YOURSELF EVERY 90
MINUTES.

BELIEVE.

BELIEVE THAT ASKING "WHY?" IS THE WAY TO REDISCOVER
YOUR TRUE HEART.

BECOME.

BECOME CONSCIOUSLY IN TUNE WITH BEING LOVE-OBSESSED. CHOOSE TO FIND LOVE IN EVERYTHING YOU DO, EVERY EXPERIENCE LIFE PRESENTS YOU, AND EVERY INTERACTION. YOU MUST REPROGRAM YOUR BRAIN BACK TO ITS ORIGINAL LOVE-FILLED STATE.

CONNECT.

YOUR HUMAN NATURE NEEDS YOU TO BE IN AN ENVIRONMENT THAT ALLOWS YOU TO FEEL LOVE FROM THE INSIDE OUT. MAKE CONSCIOUS EFFORT TO FIND THESE MOMENTS IN YOUR EVERYDAY LIFE OR SEEK OUT ONLINE COMMUNITIES, LIKE OUR SUCCESS REBEL SOCIETY, TO GET THE LOVE-FILLED GOODNESS YOU NEED.

64

90-SECOND DAILY CHECK-IN

LIVING, BEING, AND BREATHING SUCCESS ON YOUR TERMS IS ABOUT STAYING CONNECTED TO YOU AND WHAT SUCCESS IS TO YOU.

At least one time a day, run through these questions to make sure you stay grounded into what success means to you.

- What if I succeed?

- What if I influence generations?

- What if my Divine work springboards the people around me into their Divine paths and lives of NEW NOTORIETY?

- What if all of this is greater than me?

- What if this was never about me?

- What if my deeper divine message is weaving the planes of the earth and Divine in a way that I am not consciously aware of?

- What if the life of NEW NOTORIETY that my SOULFIRE sets me up for is bigger, better, and more influential, and successful than I could ever imagine?

I KNOW THE
CREATOR OF THE
UNIVERSE IS THE
CREATOR OF ME.

LEARN.

VERY FEW TRUE LIMITERS IN LIFE EXIST. THE MAJORITY OF THE TIME THERE IS ALWAYS A SOLUTION TO EVERY SITUATION. YOU JUST HAVE TO BELIEVE AND SEARCH FOR THE POSSIBILITIES.

DO.

BEGIN TO SEE THE FULL TRUTH OF THE SITUATION AT HAND, NOT JUST THE LIMITING SCOPE TOWARDS WHICH PEOPLE ARE POINTING YOU.

BELIEVE.

YOU HAVE NOT BECAUSE YOU ASK NOT. PEOPLE, THE DIVINE, AND OTHER FORCES UNSEEN WANT TO HELP YOU. BE VULNERABLE AND ASK FOR WHAT YOU FEEL YOU NEED—BE IT SOMETHING FROM THIS SIDE OF HEAVEN OR THE OTHER SIDE: ASK AND TAKE ACTION.

BECOME.

BE SOLUTION, NOT COMPROMISED, FOCUSED. THERE IS A
SOLUTION TO EVERY PROBLEM THAT LEADS EVERYONE TO FEEL
LIKE A SUCCESSFUL WINNER. DON'T FALL FOR THE OLD LINE
THAT EVERYTHING IN LIFE IS A COMPROMISE. BE LIVING PROOF
THAT EVERY SITUATION HAS A SUCCESS FILLED SOLUTION.

CONNECT.

IT IS EASY TO LOSE SIGHT OF YOUR GRANDNESS IN THE VASTNESS OF THE UNIVERSE. TAKE TIME DAILY TO REMIND YOURSELF AND CONNECT WITH THE TRUTH THAT THE GOD WHO CREATED THE VAST GALAXIES ALSO CHOSE YOU. YOU ARE VALUABLE. YOU HAVE A PURPOSE. YOU ARE LOVED BEYOND MEASURE—AND YOU ARE MEANT TO LOVE BEYOND MEASURE.

2

YOU MUST MASTER SUCCESS, STRUGGLE, AND SEX

MY SOUL ALWAYS LIVES FREE NO MATTER WHERE I MAY BE.

LEARN.

A ONE-TIME CHOICE TO STEP INTO YOUR SOULFIRE AND DIVINE PARTNERSHIP ISN'T GOING TO KEEP THE OTHERS AT BAY. THEIR ATTACKS WILL INCREASE, AND THEY WILL FORCE YOU TO DECIDE: YOU OR THEM.

DO.

WRITE YOUR INTENTIONS FOR EVERY ACTION YOU TAKE—
EVEN SMALL ONES. WHEN YOU WRITE WHAT YOUR HEART
PURPOSE IS FOR, IN THAT MOMENT YOU CREATE A MORE
POWERFUL EXPERIENCE FOR YOU AND ALL WHO ARE
INVOLVED. YOU WILL ALSO KEEP YOURSELF FOCUSED IF THE
OTHERS TRY TO MESS WITH YOU.

BELIEVE.

NEVER FORGET THAT YOU, YOUR SOULFIRE, YOUR DIVINE
PARTNERSHIP—ALL OF THIS MATTERS.

BECOME.

BEGIN TO TAKE STEPS BACK FROM DIFFICULT CONVERSATIONS. DISCERNMENT IS THE KEY TO UNDERSTANDING WHY THE FLOW ISN'T HAPPENING IN A PARTICULAR SITUATION. IS IT BECAUSE YOUR INTENTIONS ARE MISMATCHED? IS IT BECAUSE YOU HAVE A SOCIAL STORY THAT IS LIMITING YOU FROM SEEING THE TRUTH? OR ARE THE OTHERS AT PLAY IN A BIGGER WAY. TAKING A MENTAL, EMOTIONAL, SPIRITUAL, AND SOMETIMES PHYSICAL STEPS BACK FROM A SITUATION IS THE KEY TO BUILD UP YOUR ABILITY TO PROPERLY DISCERN WHAT IS TRULY HAPPENING.

CONNECT.

THOUGH IT IS HUMAN NATURE TO WANT AND NEED PHYSICAL, EMOTIONAL, AND SPIRITUAL CONNECTION, YOU HAVE TO LEARN HOW TO CONNECT WITH YOURSELVES, YOUR SOULFIRE, AND DIVINE PARTNERSHIP FIRST. BECAUSE THESE ARE THREE CONNECTIONS THAT THE OTHERS CAN NEVER TAKE AWAY FROM YOU— UNLESS YOU CHOOSE TO ABANDON THEM.

90 SECONDS
SCHEDULE YOUR INTENTIONS

I KNOW THAT MY
HEART IS MY
GREATEST ASSET.

LEARN.

JUST LIKE WITH YOUR HEART, YOU ARE STRONG AND
BEAUTIFUL. YOU HAVE A UNIQUE FLOW AND SYSTEM THAT IS
DIVINELY YOURS. TRUE SUCCESS, INFLUENCE, AND REACH WILL
HAPPEN ONCE YOU CHOOSE TO DISCOVER AND WORK IN YOUR
UNIQUE FLOW.

DO.

TAKE TIME TO DISCOVER THE LOVE AND HEART YOU HAVE FOR
YOUR SOULFIRE.

BELIEVE.

YOU HAVE THE STRENGTH AND THE RESILIENCE TO FULLY
ACHIEVE, LIVE, AND APPRECIATE ALL THAT YOUR SOULFIRE
CREATES—NO MATTER WHAT ANYONE ELSE SAYS.

BECOME.

DON'T JUST SET INTENTIONS FOR WHAT YOU WANT OUT OF
EVERY TASK, SITUATION, OR EXPERIENCE. CONSCIOUSLY
CHOOSE HOW YOU WANT YOUR HEART TO SHOW UP, AS WELL
AS HOW YOU WANT YOUR LOVE TO SHOW IN THOSE
MOMENTS.

CONNECT.

WE HAVE TO UNLEARN THE MODERN WAYS OF THE OTHERS. AND BEGIN TO TRUST IN THE DIVINE FLOW THAT GOD SO EFFORTLESSLY GIVES OUR HEARTS DAILY. WE HAVE TO TRUST THAT HIS DIVINE WAYS REACH TO OUR PARTNERSHIP AND SOULFIRE WORK. COMMIT TO JOURNALING, CREATE A SMALL GROUP, OR JOIN OUR SOCIETY—SO THAT YOU CAN TRACK HOW GOD COMES THROUGH FOR YOU EVERY TIME—AS YOU RESET YOUR WORKFLOW FROM SOLO YOU TO YOUR DIVINE PARTNERSHIP.

I KNOW THAT MY VOICE IS MINE. NO ONE CONTROLS IT BUT ME.

LEARN.

WHAT YOU SAY OR DON'T SAY MATTERS TO YOUR AUDIENCE,
BUT ALSO TO YOU. DON'T LIMIT YOUR PERSPECTIVE SIMPLY
BECAUSE THE OTHERS WANT YOU TO.

DO.

Become aware of your thoughts and your words. See how often you choose to not say or edit yourself prior to speaking. Recognize the "why" behind your self-editing and course adjust based on your motive.

BELIEVE.

YOUR UNIQUE, UNEDITED PERSPECTIVE ON THE WORLD IS WHAT
THE WORLD NEEDS.

BECOME.

CHOOSE TO UNLEARN THE LIMITING COMMUNICATION PATTERNS INTO WHICH THE OTHERS HAVE INDOCTRINATED YOU —THROUGH THE IDEAS OF POLITICAL CORRECTNESS, BELOVED RELATIONSHIPS ASKING YOU TO TONE DOWN, OR YOUR LANGUAGE CHOICES NOT BEING "APPROPRIATE."

CONNECT.

TAKE THE TIME TO CONNECT WITH YOUR UNIQUE DIVINE PERSPECTIVE. BEGIN TO JOURNAL, WRITE, AND THEN SPEAK IN AN AUTHENTIC MANNER THROUGH THE SOULFIRE TRUTH THAT LIVES INSIDE YOU.

I KNOW THAT
INNOCENT-
SOUNDING DOESN'T
MEAN INNOCENT
INTENTIONS.

LEARN.

YOU CAN'T TRUST HOW PEOPLE DESCRIBE THEMSELVES OR THEIR WORK WITHOUT FIRST BEING CLEAR ABOUT THEIR INTENTIONS.

DO.

OBJECTIVELY RUN THROUGH YOUR STORIES OF SUCCESS TO DISCOVER WHAT HIDDEN EXPECTATIONS YOU UNKNOWINGLY HAVE AND, WHICH ARE IN TURN STOPPING YOU FROM GETTING WHAT YOU WANT.

BELIEVE.

YOUR INTENTIONS CREATE YOUR ABILITY TO INFLUENCE.

BECOME.

BECOME PROACTIVE IN WHAT YOU FEED YOUR MIND. FROM THE BOOKS YOU READ TO THE MOVIES AND TELEVISION YOU WATCH—EVERYONE AND EVERYTHING HAS ITS OWN MOTIVE AND INTENTION. IF YOU AREN'T CLEAR ABOUT THEIRS YOU MAY END UP BEING CONSUMED BY THEM.

CONNECT.

CHOOSE TO REWRITE YOUR STORY, YOUR PATTERNS, AND YOUR EXPECTATIONS. YOU CONTROL YOUR OWN NARRATIVE NO MATTER WHAT THE OTHERS SAY.

90 SECOND SUCCESS LIST

Use the space below to write out all of your markers of success. You know—those moments, which in your mind mean that you have made it.

Then—come back and answer the questions, which fill in the detail as well as uncover the hidden stories of what success means to you. Highlight the areas that hold stories you want to consciously change.

SUCCESS #1:

_____

_____

_____

_____

_____

What does it mean to you to achieve this?

_____
_____
_____
_____
_____
_____

What will you look like?

_____
_____
_____
_____
_____

What will you feel like?

_____
_____
_____
_____
_____
_____
_____
_____
_____

How will you act?

_____
_____
_____
_____
_____
_____

What will you say and what will you sound like?

_____
_____
_____
_____

Who and what will be around you?

_____
_____
_____
_____

How do people react to you?

_____
_____
_____
_____
_____
_____

SUCCESS #2:

_____

_____

_____

_____

What does it mean to you to achieve this?

_____

_____

_____

_____

What will you look like?

_____

_____

_____

_____

What will you feel like?

_____

_____

_____

_____

_____

How will you act?

_____

_____

_____

_____

_____

What will you say and what will you sound like?

_____

_____

_____

_____

_____

Who and what will be around you?

_____

_____

_____

_____

_____

How do people react to you?

_____

_____

_____

_____

_____

SUCCESS #3:

_____

_____

_____

_____

_____

What does it mean to you to achieve this?

_____

_____

_____

_____

What will you look like?

_____

_____

_____

_____

What will you feel like?

_____

_____

_____

_____

How will you act?

_____

_____

_____

_____

_____

What will you say and what will you sound like?

_____

_____

_____

_____

_____

Who and what will be around you?

_____

_____

_____

_____

_____

How do people react to you?

_____

_____

_____

_____

_____

SUCCESS #4:

_____

_____

_____

_____

_____

What does it mean to you to achieve this?

_____

_____

_____

_____

_____

What will you look like?

_____

_____

_____

_____

_____

What will you feel like?

_____

_____

_____

_____

_____

How will you act?

_____

_____

_____

_____

_____

What will you say and what will you sound like?

_____

_____

_____

_____

_____

Who and what will be around you?

_____

_____

_____

_____

_____

How do people react to you?

_____

_____

_____

_____

SUCCESS #5:

_____

_____

_____

_____

_____

What does it mean to you to achieve this?

_____

_____

_____

_____

_____

What will you look like?

_____

_____

_____

_____

_____

What will you feel like?

_____

_____

_____

_____

_____

How will you act?

_____

_____

_____

_____

_____

What will you say and what will you sound like?

_____

_____

_____

_____

_____

Who and what will be around you?

_____

_____

_____

_____

_____

How do people react to you?

_____

_____

_____

_____

_____

I AM BLIND TO ONLY
KNOW AND FOLLOW
MY OWN HEART.

LEARN.

WE CANNOT LET THE FALSEHOOD OF SCARCITY, COMPETITION, AND MIRRORING OTHERS' BEHAVIOR INVADE OUR MIND AND HEARTSCAPES.

DO.

AUDIT HOW YOU SPEND YOUR EVERYDAY LIFE. MUCH TIME, RESOURCES, AND ENERGY CAN BE WASTED—SIMPLY BECAUSE WE FULFILL THE EXPECTATIONS OF OTHERS.

BELIEVE.

YOU ARE NOT IN COMPETITION WITH ANYONE OR ANYTHING ON THIS SIDE OF HEAVEN. YOU ARE SOLELY IN PARTNERSHIP WITH THE DIVINE.

BECOME.

RECOGNIZE THAT STRUGGLE MEANS THAT YOU ARE OUT OF
ALIGNMENT WITH YOUR DIVINE PARTNERSHIP OR SOULFIRE.

CONNECT.

MANY OF US HAVE GROWN UP WITH THE BELIEFS THAT
"SUCCESS IS HARD" AND "MONEY DOESN'T GROW ON TREES."
FIND A COMMUNITY OF NEW PEOPLE WHOM YOU CAN HANG
OUT WITH IN PERSON AND/OR ONLINE. MONITOR WHAT YOU
READ AND WATCH AS ENTERTAINMENT, SO YOU DON'T
REINFORCE OLD BELIEFS.

3

**DECIDE IF YOU
ARE WITH THE
OTHERS OR ARE
YOU AN
OUTCAST**

I KNOW FROM THE DEPTHS OF MY CORE THAT I AM UNCONDITIONALLY LOVED AND WANTED.

LEARN.

IF YOU DON'T LOVE IT, YOU WILL NEVER BE TRULY SUCCESSFUL
AT IT.

DO.

STOP FOCUSING ON YOUR SUCCESS "TO DO" LIST AND FOCUS INSTEAD ON WHAT SETS YOUR HEART ON FIRE.

BELIEVE.

BELIEVE THAT YOUR HEART WILL NEVER LEAD YOU ASTRAY.

CONNECT.

ENGAGE WITH PEOPLE WHO HAVE SIMILAR PASSIONS AND SEE
THE WORLD YOUR WAY.

**WITHOUT LOVING
MYSELF FIRST,
NOTHING ELSE CAN
SUCCEED.**

LEARN.

YOUR SUCCESS OR FAILURE BEGINS IN YOUR MIND.

DO.

START DAYDREAMING INTENTIONALLY TO OVERCOME THE STRONGHOLDS THAT HAVE BEEN EMBEDDED IN YOU—AND BEGIN TO PROPEL YOUR SOULFIRE FORWARD.

BELIEVE.

YOUR MIND IS MORE POWERFUL THAN YOU KNOW.

BECOME.

BEGIN TO ACT, SPEAK, DRESS, BEHAVE, THINK, AND REACT AS
THE PERSON YOU SEE IN YOUR MIND'S EYE. CHOOSING SUCH
ACTIONS CONSCIOUSLY WILL PROPEL YOUR SUCCESS INTO THE
LIFE OF NEW NOTORIETY.

CONNECT.

CONSCIOUSLY INVESTIGATE THE STRONGHOLDS THAT MAY BE HOLDING YOU BACK AND CONNECT WITH LIKE-MINDED PEOPLE WHO SPEAK THE TRUTH ABOUT THEIR STRONGHOLDS AND HOW THEY POSITIVELY MOVE FORWARD.

THE HURT THAT IS MEANT TO HARM ME NEVER HIT MY HEART.

LEARN.

HURTS HAPPEN IN LIFE, BUT IT IS HOW WE HEAL THAT CREATES
TRUE TRANSFORMATION.

DO.

WE ALL HAVE PAIN. WE ALL HAVE HURTS. BEGIN TO ACTIVELY
REFRAME THEM SO THAT YOU CAN BREAK FREE OF THE HOLDS
THE OTHERS HAVE ON YOU.

BELIEVE.

YOU ARE FULLY CAPABLE OF OVERCOMING EVERY PAIN, EVERY
HURT THAT COMES YOUR WAY. AND YES, I KNOW THAT SUCKS
WHEN YOU ARE IN THE MIDDLE OF ALL OF IT!

BECOME.

PAIN WILL ALWAYS HAPPEN ON THIS SIDE OF HEAVEN, YET WHEN WE STAY IN THE FLOW OF OUR SOULFIRE AND ARE COMMITTED TO OUR DIVINE PARTNERSHIP, THE PAIN IS MORE PALATABLE.

CONNECT.

TALK AND MOVE ON. FIND A GREAT THERAPIST, FRIEND, OR
YOUR CAT—AND TALK IT OUT. WHEN YOU VERBALIZE HOW
YOU FEEL YOU ARE ABLE TO RELEASE NOT JUST THE THOUGHTS,
BUT THE ENERGETICS OF THE EXPERIENCE AS WELL.

EVERY OBSTACLE ACCELERATES MY SUCCESS.

LEARN.

YOU ARE IN TOTAL CONTROL ON HOW YOU REACT.

DO.

WHEN SITUATIONS COME ASK YOUR DIVINE PARTNER, "DO I PUSH OR PULL?"

BELIEVE.

CHOOSING THE SOLUTION THAT WORKS BEST FOR YOU, NO
MATTER HOW ILLOGICAL IT LOOKS, IS STILL THE RIGHT CHOICE
FOR YOU.

BECOME.

TUNE INTO YOUR AWARENESS OF THE BIGGER SITUATION AT HAND. STOP BEING REACTIONARY IN THE MOMENT AND LOOK AT THE BIGGER LANDSCAPE—THE BIGGER STORY AT PLAY. BECOME THE PERSON WHO TAKES UNAPOLOGETIC DECISIVE ACTION ON WHEN TO PUSH AND WHEN TO PAUSE.

CONNECT.

PRACTICE MAKES PERFECT, BUT LET'S BE HONEST—YOU REALLY DON'T WANT TO HAVE TO PRACTICE THIS ALL THAT MUCH. FIND A COMMUNITY OF LIKE-MINDED PEOPLE WHO OPENLY MODEL BEST BEHAVIORS SO THAT YOU CAN LEARN FROM OTHERS, VS. JUST YOUR ACTIONS.

PUSH AND PULL

Whenever you feel like you are facing an obstacle or are overwhelmed about what the next step is to take, take the following actions.

PUSH. Check in with yourself and see if you can pinpoint what is going on. Are you tired? Run down? Not following through. In short, is your hesitation due to something you are not doing? Is your hesitation due to fear? Do you have self-doubt, imposter syndrome?

PAUSE. Are you moving too quickly? Do you feel out of control?

Take action and stick with it.

THE DREAMS OF MY BIRTH ALWAYS LIGHT UP MY SOUL.

LEARN.

THE INNOCENCE OF YOUR YOUTH CAN GIVE YOU THE BIGGEST INSIGHTS TO THE REAL YOU.

DO.

AUDIT YOUR LOVES FROM YOUR FIRST MEMORIES AND THEN
MOVE FORWARD FROM YOUR EARLIEST LOVES TO PRESENT
DAY. WHEN YOU UNDERSTAND THE "WHY" THAT HAS
INTUITIVELY DRIVEN YOU ALL THESE YEARS, THEN YOU WILL
UNDERSTAND THE "WHY" TO YOUR SOULFIRE WORK.

BELIEVE.

YOUTHFUL INNOCENCE DOESN'T HAVE TO EQUATE TO
IGNORANCE. INNOCENCE CAN EQUAL DIVINE INTELLIGENCE.

BECOME.

BE BOLD ENOUGH TO FOLLOW THE ROOTS OF YOUR DREAMS—
AND DETERMINED ENOUGH TO DEVELOP THEM INTO
EXPERIENCES THAT MAKE A DIFFERENCE.

CONNECT.

SHOCKER! CONNECTION AND COMMUNITY GO HAND IN HAND—ONCE YOU RECONNECT WITH YOUR SOULFIRE AND BEGIN TO TAKE STEPS IN EXPLORING WHAT THAT LOOKS LIKE AND FEELS LIKE IN YOUR LIFE TODAY. SHARE THE EMOTIONS THAT COME FORTH WITH A GROUP OF LIKE-MINDED PEOPLE WHO WON'T JUDGE, CONDEMN, OR GIVE ADVICE, BUT INSTEAD WILL HOLD THE SPACE FOR YOU TO GROW. THAT IS WHAT THE SUCCESS REBEL SOCIETY IS ALL ABOUT AND THAT IS EXACTLY WHY I CREATED IT. I CAN ONLY HOLD THE SPACE FOR SO MANY, BUT TOGETHER WE CAN HOLD THE SPACE FOR THE MASSES.

I KNOW THAT I AM FULLY CAPABLE.

LEARN.

THE REAL YOU HAS MORE DEPTH THAN THE CURRENT PATTERNS, MINDSETS, AND HABITS YOU LIVE BY. WHEN YOU UNDERSTAND YOUR NERI PROFILE, YOU EMPOWER YOURSELF TO CHOOSE A DIFFERENT HABIT, DIFFERENT MINDSET, DIFFERENT PATTERN, DIFFERENT PERSPECTIVE—EACH THAT IS INNATELY YOU.

DO.

DELVE DEEP INTO THE POSSIBILITIES THAT YOU ARE. THE NERI
WEBSITE (HTTP://NERI.IO) HAS MANY FREE RESOURCES THAT
WILL ALLOW YOU TO UNDERSTAND YOUR UNIQUE NERI MAKE
UP. ROLE PLAY IN YOUR MIND HOW YOU WILL ACT, BE, THINK,
AND BEHAVE DIFFERENTLY THAN YOU DO TODAY, BUT IF THOSE
ACTIONS ARE WITHIN YOUR NERI PROFILE, THEY COULD
CHANGE THE OUTCOME OF THE HABITUAL CYCLES YOU FIND
YOURSELF IN.

BELIEVE.

YOU ARE MORE THAN YOUR HABITS.

BECOME.

BECOME A CHOOSER. CHOOSE HOW YOU SHOW UP. CHOOSE THE EXPERIENCES YOU WANT TO CREATE FOR YOURSELF AND FOR OTHERS. CHOOSE THE EMOTIONS YOU WANT TO FEEL. CHOOSE VS. BLINDLY FOLLOWING.

CONNECT.

"PEOPLE WATCHING" IS ONE OF THE BEST WAYS TO
UNDERSTAND THE NERI METHOD IN OTHERS—AND IN
YOURSELF.

Find a place where you can comfortably sit and watch interactions that have substance. Meaning: not just people walking quickly by on the street. Review the biological, nonverbal and style traits represented in the core NERI profiles—and hypothesize on who these people are.

This is actually one of my favorite things to do solo but is a training exercise I lead during many of the boutique events I run every year. It's amazing what you can discern from people when you understand the possibilities that lie within.

NERI
WHAT ROOTS
YOUR PASSION

NO MATTER IF YOU INTEND TO BUILD YOUR STARTUP INTO A LEGACY BRAND, A SELLABLE CORPORATION, OR JUST HAVING SOME FINANCIAL FUN IN THE MOMENT—YOU ARE THE COMMON THREAD. YOU MUST LIKE AND ENJOY THIS BUSINESS AT LEAST IN THE MOMENT TO INVEST YOUR TIME, ENERGY, AND RESOURCES INTO IT.

What is it about this project that has your passions going?

_____

_____

_____

_____

_____

_____

If you are unsure, you better find some clarity quickly. Because without clarity most likely your thrill-seeking interest will fade fast, and your efforts will be for naught.

One way to find the clarity you need is to understand what drives your passion from a personality perspective. Neuro Emotional Relationship Intelligence (NERI) uses your biology, psychological programing, subconscious perceptions, and relational triggers to best understand what drives and motivates you in life.

The cool thing is that once you know your unique combination (typically a blend of 2-3 of the profiles) you can clearly see what about your startup has your juices flowing. What it also shows you is how to best keep yourself in the creative flow, and not get bored or burnt out.

Want to know what NERI combination you are? Take the quiz to learn how your passions are rooted. https://neriquiz.com

I KNOW THAT I AM UNIQUELY DESIGNED FOR THIS.

LEARN.

YOUR DEFINITION OF SUCCESS IS THE ONLY ONE THAT
MATTERS. YOUR DEFINITION NEEDS TO BE CLEAR, TACTICAL,
AND TANGIBLE. YES, IT CAN HAVE ALL THE FEELS, BUT YOU
HAVE TO KNOW WHEN YOU HAVE "MADE IT."

DO.

THERE ARE MANY FACTORS THAT EITHER BRING A TRAIT FORWARD OR SUPPRESS IT. IF YOU AREN'T SEEING THE RESULTS YOU WANT, EVALUATE EVERYONE AND ANYTHING THAT IS AROUND AS WELL AS INSIDE YOU. JUST LIKE WITH YOUR DNA, HAVING YOU SHIFT FROM STRUGGLE TO SUCCESS IS JUST LIKE FLIPPING A SWITCH.

BELIEVE.

JUST BECAUSE YOU HAVEN'T DOESN'T MEAN THAT YOU CAN'T.

_____
_____
_____
_____
_____
_____
_____
_____
_____
_____
_____
_____
_____
_____
_____
_____
_____
_____
_____
_____
_____
_____
_____
_____

BECOME.

MAKE FAITH THE POINT FROM WHICH EVERYTHING YOU DO,
SAY, OR THINK COMES FROM. BE A PERSON THAT BELIEVES
EVERYTHING IS POSSIBLE.

CONNECT.

SURROUND YOURSELF WITH PEOPLE, BOOKS, TRAINING, SHOWS, THAT STIR UP THAT "NEVER SAY DIE." ATTITUDE. USE TECHNOLOGY TO YOUR ADVANTAGE TO KEEP YOUR MIND FOCUSED ON WHAT YOU REALLY WANT.

I KNOW THAT EVERY DREAM, HOPE, AND DESIRE CAN BE MY REALITY IN AN INSTANT.

LEARN.

YOUR MIND AND IMAGINATION CAN EITHER BE YOUR SECRET
TOOLS TO RIDICULOUS SUCCESS OR NEVER-ENDING
SABOTAGE.

DO.

PAUSE AND HONESTLY EVALUATE WHAT IS TRULY HOLDING
YOU BACK. THE MORE THAT IT IS YOU, THE BETTER THAT IS,
BECAUSE YOU CAN CHANGE YOURSELF MUCH EASIER AND
FASTER THAN AN EXTERNAL SITUATION, WHICH INVOLVES
OTHERS.

BELIEVE.

EVERYTHING IS POSSIBLE.

BECOME.

REALIZE THAT YOUR SUCCESS GOES FAR GREATER THAN YOU. WHEN YOU ARE ABLE TO BREAK FREE FROM THE SOCIAL STORIES AND CONTROL OF THE OTHERS—YOU MAKE YOUR LIFE BETTER. BUT YOU ALSO SHOW EVERYONE AROUND WHAT IS POSSIBLE IN THEIR OWN LIVES.

Find ways to stay grounded in your Soulfire and Divine Partnership on a daily basis. Some people use active journaling while others use guided meditation. When you find the ways, which make your partnership feel palatable, you will be able to keep mental strength and clarity on point.

Start today being the ink writer—not pencil scheduler. Start today being the person who is known for their "Yes's" meaning "Yes" and their "No's" meaning "No."

CONNECT

THERE WILL BE MOMENTS WHEN DRAWING LINES IN THE CONCRETE SIMPLY ISN'T FUN. THERE WILL BE DAYS WHEN YOU WANT TO PUSH BACK YOUR DEADLINE OR FORGIVE, ONE MORE TIME, A FRIEND WHO FLAKED ON YOU. EVERY TIME YOU WANT TO MOVE THE LINE IN THE CONCRETE YOU HAVE TO ASK YOURSELF "WHY?" AND ANSWER THE QUESTION HONESTLY. IS IT BECAUSE YOU MISCALCULATED YOUR TIME OR IS IT BECAUSE IT WASN'T A PRIORITY?

Becoming a line in the concrete person with yourself, your business, and the people you won't make you the most popular, but you will be unapologetically known for being a person of your word and consistent through and through. And as with everything, you will find people to hang out with that also share these qualities. If it is through the Success Rebel Society or just with like-minded "get'er done" types of peeps. The company you keep greatly impacts the consistency of your success and growth.

MY SOULFIRE ALWAYS BURNS AS BRIGHT AS THE NORTH STAR.

LEARN.

SUCCESS ONLY COMES WHEN TRUTH IS AT THE FOUNDATION.

DO.

GET RIDICULOUSLY HONEST ABOUT HOW YOU WANT YOUR LIFE TO GO. CLEAR OUT SUBCONSCIOUS STORIES THAT ARE HOLDING YOU BACK. MAKE CONSCIOUS EFFORT—BEGIN TO USE YOUR SUBCONSCIOUS MIND TO YOUR FULL ADVANTAGE.

BELIEVE.

Believe what you say you want and who you say you are.

184

BECOME.

GUARD YOUR HEART AND YOUR MIND FROM FRIVOLOUS
SOCIAL STORIES, WHICH MAY SEEM BENIGN BUT GO AGAINST
THE LIFE YOU WANT TO LEAD, HOW YOU VIEW YOURSELF, AND
HOW YOU SEE THE WORK OF YOUR SOULFIRE.

CONNECT.

LIKE WITH ALL LIFE CHANGING TRANSFORMATIONS, YOU HAVE TO SURROUND YOURSELF WITH PEOPLE AND SOCIAL STORIES THAT SUPPORT YOUR PERSPECTIVE. RECOVERING ALCOHOLICS DON'T GO BACK AND HANG OUT IN BARS. AND PEOPLE LOOKING TO LIVE THEIR SOULFIRE, BECOME INFLUENCERS, AND LIVE A LIFE OF NEW NOTORIETY CAN'T HANG OUT WITH THE SAME PEOPLE WHO CREATED THE SUBCONSCIOUS MENTAL BLOCKS THAT WERE STOPPING THEM IN THE FIRST PLACE.

I KNOW THAT I AM NEVER STUCK. THERE IS ALWAYS A SOLUTION.

LEARN.

THE SIMPLEST SOLUTIONS CAN CREATE RADICAL RESULTS
WHEN PURPOSEFUL ACTION IS TAKEN.

DO.

COMMIT YOURSELF TO BEING SOLUTION FOCUSED VS. METHOD FOCUSED. BE OPEN TO THE CREATIVE IDEAS THAT PAUSE. PLAN. PIVOT CAN GIVE YOU—THE "HOW" TO BRING YOUR SOULFIRE AND THE WORK OF YOUR DIVINE PARTNERSHIP INTO THE WORLD.

BELIEVE.

SUCCESS IS JUST A SOLUTION AWAY.

BECOME.

BECOME KNOWN AS A SOLUTIONIST PERSON; WHEN YOU SEE
THE SOLUTIONS, YOU SEE THE POSSIBILITIES.

CONNECT.

BEING SOLUTION MINDED REQUIRES THAT YOU TRAIN YOUR BRAIN TO SEE. PLAY SUDOKU AND OTHER PROBLEM-SOLVING GAMES. PERSONALLY, MY FAVORITE APP FOR THIS IS CALLED LUMOSITY. IT HAS BEEN AROUND FOR YEARS; IT HAS A VARIETY OF GAMES TO HELP KEEP YOUR MIND SHARP AND YOUR SOLUTION FOCUSED BRAIN ON POINT.

PAUSE. PLAN. PIVOT.

PAUSE, PLAN, AND PIVOT IS ABOUT RECOGNIZING AND COURSE CORRECTING WHEN YOU HAVE GOTTEN OFF TRACK FROM YOUR SOULFIRE, DIVINE PARTNERSHIP, AND THE LIFE OF GRACE, SUCCESS, INFLUENCE, AND NEW NOTORIETY. YOU ARE MEANT TO LIVE. AND THEN—CONSCIOUSLY PIVOTING AND TAKING ACTION WITH NEW CLARITY, INTENTION, PURPOSE, AND IN PARTNERSHIP.

Like all the "rules" in this book, the hardest part isn't taking action; it is trusting yourself that your instinct was right, sound, and accurate for you. But when done right the PAUSE, PLAN and PIVOT method transforms.

PAUSE. Take a deep breath and recognize where you are at and where you want to be.
PLAN. If the purpose or "why" behind your actions is still real, then explore new ways of how you can still achieve your "why."

PIVOT. With your "why" re-inspired, start to take action, but keep your eye on your "why."

I KNOW THAT REBELS ARE MEANT TO BE REVOLUTIONARY.

LEARN.

YOU MAY NOT BE ABLE TO CONTROL HOW OTHERS BEHAVE,
BUT YOU CONTROL THE GAME YOU PLAY.

DO.

BEING A SUCCESS REBEL ISN'T ALWAYS ABOUT FIGHTING THE
"GOOD FIGHT" AGAINST THE OTHERS. SOMETIMES IT IS AS
SIMPLE AS USING THEIR OWN GAME TO YOUR ADVANTAGE.
BEGIN TO LOOK AT THE GAME THEY ARE TRYING TO PLAY WITH
YOU AND SEE HOW YOU CAN USE IT TO YOUR ADVANTAGE.

BELIEVE.

IF YOU CONTROL YOUR MIND, YOU CONTROL YOUR DESTINY.

BECOME.

LEARN HOW TO TAKE A STEP BACK AND OBJECTIVELY EVALUATE THE MOVES YOU ARE MAKING. ARE YOU LEAVING YOURSELF OPEN IN A CERTAIN AREA? NOT COMING ACROSS AS POWERFUL AS YOU COULD BE WITH THE IMPRESSIONS YOU ARE MAKING? ALLOWING OTHERS TO MARGINALIZE YOU IN SOME WAY?

CONNECT.

BY LEARNING HOW TO TAKE A MENTAL STEP BACK FROM THE SITUATION, YOU CAN PROPERLY ORCHESTRATE THE MOVES YOU MAKE AND HOW YOU CAN USE THE MOVES OF THE OTHERS AGAINST THEMSELVES.

Yes, being a Success Rebel can be exhausting. Sometimes you just need real human interaction. This is why with both the Success Rebel Society and the Success Rebel CEO Life group we have in person experiences and meet ups all around the world. They are great ways to grow, learn, and simply chill in like mindedness.

I NEVER LOSE SIGHT OF MY "WHY" BECAUSE I BECOME OBSESSED WITH THE "HOW."

LEARN.

YOU ARE MULTIFACETED AND WHAT YOU PURSUE SHOULD BE TOO. STICKING TO ONE AREA FOR THE SAKE OF FOLLOWING THE RULES WILL ONLY LEAD TO FAILURE.

DO.

STOP FOCUSING ON THE ONE. THE ONE WAY TO SUCCEED. THE ONE WAY TO MAKE MONEY. THE ONE WAY TO FIND ONE. CREATE THE FRAMEWORK NECESSARY TO MAKE SURE YOU WIN IN ALL AREAS OF YOUR LIFE, WHILE STILL ACHIEVING THE GOAL YOU ARE GOING AFTER.

BELIEVE.

"HOW" SUCCESS SHOWS UP IS LESS IMPORTANT THAN "WHY"
THE SUCCESS APPEARS.

BECOME.

BECOME OBSESSED WITH YOUR VISION. DON'T LET ANYONE LIMIT YOUR REACH, SCOPE, OR INFLUENCE SIMPLY BECAUSE SOMETHING ISN'T "INDUSTRY STANDARD." CHANGE THE STANDARD, CHANGE THE INDUSTRY, UP-LEVEL YOUR INFLUENCE.

CONNECT.

MANY TIMES, SUCCESS REBELS USE THEIR SOULFIRES AND DIVINE PARTNERSHIPS—NOT JUST AS WAYS TO CHANGE THE WORLD—BUT REVENUE MAKERS AS WELL. TO KEEP SUCH GROWTH UP IN A HIGH INTENSITY, LOW COMPETITION MANNER IS A CHALLENGE WHEN YOU ARE WORKING SOLO.

This is one reason why along with my production company, we created Success Rebel CEO Life. This intimate in person group is a marketing, media, influence building program. But the byproduct of that is a community of fellow, driven success rebels who inspire, spark ideas, and encourage—but don't compete.

I KNOW THE POWER OF CONSISTENCY.

LEARN.

THE MEANING OF SOCIAL STORIES AND STEREOTYPES CHANGE
BASED ON THE NEEDS OF THE OTHERS. THE SAME HOLDS TRUE
OF THE IMMEDIATE GRATIFICATION FOR INFLUENCE, INCOME,
AND INSTANT SUCCESS. CONSISTENCY—THE KARMA SUTRA
OF SUCCESS—IS WHERE GROWTH, TRUE INFLUENCE, AND THE
LIFE OF NEW NOTORIETY COME FROM.

DO.

COMMIT TO THE LONG-TERM GAME, THE LONG-TERM SUCCESS,
AND LONG-TERM INFLUENCE THAT WILL GAIN YOU THE
RELATIONSHIPS, INFLUENCE, AND SUCCESS YOU WANT.

BELIEVE.

CONSISTENCY IN THE END WINS.

BECOME.

YOUR SOULFIRE WON'T BE FULLY REALIZED IN A DAY. LEARN
THE ART OF PIVOTING FROM THE BIG VISION, GOALS, AND
DREAMS YOU HAVE AND THE STEPS YOU KNOW WHEN DONE
CONSISTENTLY WILL GET YOU THERE. WITHIN YOUR DIVINE
PARTNERSHIP YOU ARE THE HANDS AND FEET, SO TRYING TO
SPRINT TO THE FINISH LINE WILL ONLY LEAVE YOU WORN OUT.
BE INSPIRED BY THE OVERARCHING MISSION OF YOUR
SOULFIRE AND COMMIT TO TAKE ONE STEP FORWARD EVERY
DAY TOWARD IT.

CONNECT.

IT IS HARD TO FEEL CONSISTENT WHEN YOU FEEL LIKE YOU ARE TAKING TWO STEPS FORWARD AND THREE STEPS BACK. MANY TIMES, IT ISN'T THE PROBLEMS IN THE PHYSICAL WORLD THAT ARE STOPPING US. IT IS THE INFLUENCE OF THE OTHERS' ENERGY AND ATTACKS FROM THE SPIRITUAL WORLD THAT SLOW US DOWN TO A CRAWL.

I have always been a big proponent for Prayer Warriors. Prayer Warriors are a group of people who are dedicated to praying for you, your business, your relationships, your life overall. Personally, Success Rebels tend to have an empathic side to their personality. Therefore, negative feelings, emotions, and energies can get them off track. And creating a hard-shell exterior, which blocks them from their true brilliance. This is where the Prayer Warriors come in.

And it is one reason why every month in the Success Rebel Society, I lead a live Prayer Warrior call where we pray for and over each other's SOULFIREs, while sharing the success stories that have occurred along the way.

PRAYER WARRIOR LIST

Take the time to write down your big dreams, your big visions, and what your Divine partnership is all about for you. Share your list with people you trust and ask for their energy and prayers towards your big vision.

On the right side of the column, write the list of prayers you are holding for others.

Review your lists daily and write next to each prayer when you see progress.

5

**BE UTTERLY
SELFISH TO BE
OF SERVICE
AND A SUCCESS**

I KNOW THAT TRUE CURRENCY AND VALUE IS IN THE ENERGY I BRING.

LEARN.

WHEN YOU WORK AND LIVE FROM A PLACE OF YOUR SOULFIRE
AND DIVINE PARTNERSHIP THE VALUE OF YOUR WORK IS NOT
IN HOW IT MANIFESTS. IT IS IN THE ENERGY THAT YOUR WORK
BRINGS TO THE WORLD THAT HOLDS THE VALUE.

DO.

KEEP A RUNNING LIST OF WHAT, WHO, AND HOW YOUR
ENERGY GETS DRAINED THROUGHOUT THE DAY.

Does hearing the sound of you receiving a text message make you feel anxious? Does getting an email from a particular client or your mother-in-law make you want to run away and become a server at a small diner in rural Montana where no one and no technology can find you?
Track it and then take action to protect your energy at all costs.

BELIEVE.

It isn't "what" you do that makes you wanted. It is the energy in which you do it.

BECOME.

BE SELFISH ABOUT HOW, WITH WHOM, AND WHERE YOU PUT YOUR ENERGY. IT IS YOUR RESPONSIBILITY AS THE HANDS AND FEET IN YOUR DIVINE PARTNERSHIP TO MAKE SURE THAT YOUR ENERGY IS ALWAYS BRINGING YOUR A-GAME. DUMP THE FRIENDS, CLIENTS, AND CO-WORKERS WHOSE ENERGETIC DRAMA IS BRINGING YOU DOWN. SELFISHNESS ABOUT YOUR ENERGY IS THE KEY TO YOUR ULTIMATE SUCCESS.

CONNECT.

FIND PLACES AND HOBBIES THAT ALLOW YOU TO GROUND
YOUR ENERGY WHILE RENEWING YOUR SOUL. FOR EXAMPLE,
WALKING BAREFOOT IN THE GRASS FOR 20 MINUTES ON A
SUNNY DAY IS AN EASY WAY TO GROUND YOUR ENERGY AND
YOUR BIORHYTHMS TOO. BEST OF ALL, IT'S FREE.

DRAMA FREE ZONE LIST

Mark this page and keep a running list of what actions, people, obligations, and situations that drain or shift your energy in a negative way. Logical or not, write it down on the column to the left. Walk away, and when you return use the column to the right to write down how you can edit, end, or reimagine what is creating the drama.

KNOW THAT MYSELF AND LIFE ARE LIKE A MULTIFACETED PRISM: BEAUTIFUL, AWE INSPIRING AND ONE.

LEARN.

THERE IS NO SUBSTITUTE OR FAST HACK TO THE DIVINE
PARTNERSHIP YOUR HEART AND MIND SEEK.

DO.

AS YOU WRITE OUT THE INTENTION FOR EVERY ACTION YOU TAKE EACH DAY GO ONE STEP FURTHER AND ASK YOURSELF, "HOW DOES THIS AFFECT YOU AND YOUR DIVINE PARTNERSHIP?"

Is the act an antiquated and poor substitute to the deeper relationship you seek? Is it an act that brings your SOULFIRE and DIVINE PARTNERSHIP into this world?

When you understand not just "why" behind your action, but the Divine connection, too, you are able to not just do every act in your day with purpose and passion, but you can also find personal fulfillment in an entirely new light.

BELIEVE.

YOUR MIND IS MORE POWERFUL THAN YOU FULLY REALIZE. PROTECT IT AT ALL COST.

BECOME.

WHEN WE STEP BACK AND LOOK AT THE BEINGS THAT WE ARE.
WE ARE VERY MULTIFACETED ON A BIOLOGICAL LEVEL ALONE.
YET WE DARE THINK TO BRING THIS MULTIFACETED PERSPECTIVE
INTO OUR RELATIONSHIPS, OUR WORK, OUR CAREERS, OUR
LIVES —WE ARE TOLD HOW CONFUSING THAT WOULD BE. THAT
NO ONE WOULD UNDERSTAND WHO WE ARE. PEOPLE
COULDN'T RELATE.

Become the multifaceted person that you truly
are in every situation. Embrace the totality that
is. And use the depths of who you are
intelligently throughout every day of your life.
People won't get confused by who you are and
what you are about. They will actually find it
refreshing and relatable because they too are
multifaceted.

CONNECT.

THE BEST WAY TO PUT THIS INTO ACTION IS WITH NERI. IT SHOWS YOU ALL THE POSSIBILITIES THAT ARE UNIQUE TO YOUR PERSONALITY AND THEN ALLOWS YOU TO TAKE INTELLIGENT ACTION BY BRINGING YOUR MULTIFACETED SELF TO ALL THAT YOU DO.

WHO I AM

Based off your unique NERI profile, The following include a snapshot about what drives you and others.

NEURO

EMOTIONAL

RELATIONSHIP

INTELLIGENCE

NEW YORK CITY

OVERALL:

Direct
Passionate
Others won't get in their way
Clear communicator

STYLE:

Unique
Trendsetter
Edgy
High contrast
Bold

SOCIAL:

Extroverted and introverted
Heard before seen
Statement making
Social on purpose
Business/passion first

MINDSET:

Driven
Clear and focused
Unstoppable
List maker
Constant learner

RELATIONSHIPS:

Knows lots of people
Connects with few
Always has a purpose
Must be win/win
Dislikes "needy" people

BUSINESS:

Risk taker
Multi-focused
Gets seen
Can be seen as pushy

NEURO
EMOTIONAL
RELATIONSHIP
INTELLIGENCE

CHARLESTON

OVERALL:

Kind to a fault
Others first
Self-sacrificing
Constant volunteer
Great listener

STYLE:

Soft and approachable
Sentimental
"Sweet"
Bright colors
Never a threat

SOCIAL:

Others first
The "Mom" to
everyone
Super positive
The "go-to" friend
Only has kind words

MINDSET:

Helper
Sweetheart
Service to others-
always
Planner
Can never be the "bad
guy"

RELATIONSHIPS:

No boundaries
Will destroy self for
others
Nurturer
Sentimental
attachments
Ultimate giver

BUSINESS:

Underprices
themselves
Not about them
Service first
All about the
relationships
Not about the money

NEURO
EMOTIONAL
RELATIONSHIP
INTELLIGENCE

BOSTON

OVERALL:

Structure
Systems
Boundaries
Logical
Not outwardly emotional

STYLE:

Structured
Classic style
Business colors
Understated
Never uber casual

SOCIAL:

Structure
Clear outcomes and
boundaries
Classic roles
No extreme emotions
Always professional

MINDSET:

Loves classic learning
Expert in their focus
Loves clarity
Loves "to-do" lists
9-5 mindset

RELATIONSHIPS:

Defined expectations
Never show true heart
Different versions of
them depending on the
relationship
Social protocols and
boundaries
Never vulnerable

BUSINESS:

Knows systems and
structures
Classic communication
methods
Time frames
Over-communicates
Stays in lane

NEURO
EMOTIONAL
RELATIONSHIP
INTELLIGENCE

SEATTLE

OVERALL:

Laid back
Focused but aloof
Not structured
No timeframes
Never in a rush

STYLE:

Casual
Comfort first
Not style-focused
Can come across as
sloppy
Neutral colors

SOCIAL:

Structure
Clear outcomes and
boundaries
Classic roles
No extreme emotions
Always professional

MINDSET:

Jumps headfirst into
passion
Passions change over
time
Thinks of themselves
as the leader
Wants to be free

RELATIONSHIPS:

Can't be wrong
Don't question
Must be #1 in
relationship
Needs people to believe
in them
Committed to
themselves first

BUSINESS:

Expertise centered
"Mad genius"
Wants to focus on the
craft, not the rest
Talks "tech"
Industry leader

I KNOW THAT I AM
NEVER ALONE.

LEARN.

WORDS DON'T JUST SHAPE YOUR MIND. THEY SHAPE YOUR
CELLS, ACTIONS, INTENTIONS, AND FUTURE.

DO.

CHOOSE TODAY WHICH WORDS DO AND DO NOT DEFINE WHAT YOUR LIFE OF NEW NOTORIETY, THE RELATIONSHIPS OF YOUR DREAM, AND THE SUCCESS OF YOUR HEART MEANS TO YOU. THEN ONLY ALLOW THE WORDS ON YOUR "DO" LIST TO BE USED WHEN DISCUSSING THOSE TOPICS.

BELIEVE.

YOUR WORDS AND HOW YOU DEFINE THE WORLD DEFINE YOUR
WEALTH.

BECOME.

BECOME A TRUTH TALKER. SHARE THE POSSIBILITIES, SOLUTIONS, AND GOODNESS YOU SEE IN THE WORLD.

CONNECT.

SHARE YOUR WORDS WITH THE WORLD. SEND NOTES OF
ENCOURAGEMENT AND A JOB WELL DONE TO STRANGERS YOU
SIMPLY MEET IN PASSING. PAUSE AND TELL THE ONES YOU
LOVE HOW YOU TRULY FEEL ABOUT THEM AND THE POTENTIAL
YOU SEE IN THEM.

I KNOW THE PURITY AND DIVINITY OF MY HEART.

LEARN.

TRYING TO BE ANYTHING OTHER THAN YOUR TRUE SELF IS
POINTLESS.

DO.

INVEST IN KNOWING YOUR TRUE INTENTIONS AND
PROACTIVELY MODIFYING YOUR BEHAVIORS THAT ARE NOT IN
LINE WITH YOUR SOULFIRE, DIVINE PARTNERSHIP, AND LIFE
OF NEW NOTORIETY.

BELIEVE.

THE REAL YOU IS VALUABLE, WANTED, NEEDED, AND LOVED.

BECOME.

BECOME AN INVESTIGATOR OF THE HABITUAL ACTIONS, BEHAVIORS, AND RELATIONSHIPS YOU CREATE. LOOK FOR PATTERNS THAT NO LONGER SERVE WHERE YOUR LIFE IS GOING AND COURSE CORRECT EITHER YOUR REACTION, SITUATION, OR THE PEOPLE INVOLVED.

CONNECT.

DISCOVERING BEHAVIORAL PATTERNS THAT ARE NO LONGER
SERVING US CAN BE A CHALLENGE BECAUSE THESE PATTERNS
SHOW UP IN OUR ADULT LIFE, CAREERS, AND ASPIRATIONS
DIFFERENTLY THAN WHEN WE WERE KIDS.

Some of these learned behaviors are due to childhood trauma and others are just familiar behaviors that continue from generation to generation. One of the easiest ways to break the root of these mindsets is by changing the nonverbal communication that goes along with the habit.

ROOT OF YOUR MINDSET

Success can't come if you are stuck in the same subconscious loop. On the left column write down what patterns, emotions, feelings, situations, or relationships keep showing up in your life. Then on the right column think back to the first time you can remember this instance first appeared.

One by one journal about the people, emotions, experience, expectations, and energy around the original memory. Then literally rewrite your story to what you want it to be.

I KNOW THAT NO MATTER HOW FAR I HAVE COME, I AM CAPABLE OF SO MUCH MORE.

LEARN.

Being a Success Rebel means that you are a leader in your work, the people in your life, and the people who help bring your Soulfire to even more people than you could alone.

DO.

BE FEARLESS IN WHEN AND WHERE YOU SHOW UP BECAUSE YOUR **SOULFIRE** AND LIFE OF NEW NOTORIETY ISN'T ABOUT YOU OR FOR YOU. IT IS ABOUT THE ONES YOU SERVE.

BELIEVE.

I AM A LEADER.

BECOME.

LEADERSHIP IS A SKILL MANY ARE STRUGGLING WITH BECAUSE THEY AREN'T REALLY SURE HOW TO DO IT. FROM SOCIAL STORIES, TO POOR ROLE MODELS TO NO MODELS—ASK YOUR DIVINE PARTNERSHIP TO SHOW HOW LEADERSHIP LOOKS AND FEELS LIKE FOR YOU.

CONNECT.

LEADERSHIP IS A SKILL AND AN ART BECAUSE IN THE END IT IS A
RELATIONSHIP. FIND LEADERS THAT YOU LOVE, LEARN WHAT
THEY DO AND WHY THEY DO IT. USE YOUR NERI PROFILE TO
TRY ON LEADERSHIP STYLES THAT FIT YOUR UNIQUE PROFILE
AND SEE WHAT WORKS FOR YOU TODAY WITH WHERE YOU ARE
AT AND WHERE YOU WANT TO GO.

I KNOW THAT I AM
CAPABLE OF
ANYTHING IF I KEEP
MY MIND CLEAR AND
MY HEART PURE.

LEARN.

FOCUS ON THE FAITH IN YOUR ACTIONS AND LEARN FROM THE
RESULTS YOUR FAITH PRODUCES.

DO.

STOP FOCUSING ON THE SPECIFICITY OF THE DELIVERABLE AND START TO FOCUS ON THE INTENTION BEHIND IT.

BELIEVE.

FAITH IS WHAT CREATES SUCCESS.

BECOME.

IF YOU HAVE TAKEN ACTION ON THE PROMPTS ALL
THROUGHOUT THIS BOOK, YOU ARE ALREADY A PERSON WHO
SEES THE SOLUTIONS AROUND THEM. LET'S TAKE THAT ONE
STEP FURTHER AND BECOME THE PERSON WHO SEES THE
POTENTIAL AROUND THEM. THE POTENTIAL IN PEOPLE. THE
POTENTIAL OF YOUR WORK. THE POTENTIAL IN YOUR FAMILY.
THE POTENTIAL IN YOUR RELATIONSHIPS. THE POTENTIAL IN
WHAT YOUR DIVINE PARTNERSHIP CAN PRODUCE.

CONNECT.

BEFORE YOU JUDGE IF YOUR ACTIONS ARE A SUCCESS OR A
FAILURE PAUSE AND CONNECT WITH THE FAITH THAT STARTED IT
ALL.

SOUL TARGET: HOW TO STOP THE ENDLESS LIST OF "TO DO" AND GET STUFF DONE

If you were blessed to be born into Western society, you have built into you the desire to succeed. For many of us, success is a financial goal or professional accomplishment. Yet, to me achieving or making progress in whatever excites you to wake up in the morning is success.

No matter what your definition or goal is, the desire to achieve it is strong. And few things are stronger if you are that "Type A" driven nature.

The "Type A" personality is characterized with a drive, focus, and fearlessness "no matter what it will be" nature. It is these characteristics that makes people, like us, the natural leaders, entrepreneurs, and the solution finders of the world.

Most "Type A" s also tend to be perfectionists. Though logically unrealistic, perfectionism seems totally attainable by the "Type A" nature. We will achieve success ahead of schedule, under budget, exceeding all expectations from others, become known for such an amazing accomplishment, and do it all in a beautiful "Martha Stewart" manner.

The downside, if you want to call it that, to these amazing personality traits is that achieving success is never as satisfying as we think it is going to be. Because to us, when we do technically achieve our goal, it isn't as graceful, uber successful, or with as much fanfare we were secretly hoping for, therefore, we question if we were truly successful. And if by chance we don't hit our goal 100% spot on, then that too can be a failure as well. Did we earn our check mark? Our gold stars? If we didn't achieve the secret success we were hoping to, then, no, we didn't deserve anything though to the rest of the world we did not fail, to us we did.

If this sounds like you then you understand the battle at hand. You want to succeed in a great and glorious way. To be most effective you decide to implement a tool or strategy to help you achieve more.

You've tried it all. Traditional goal setting, the to-do list, the vision board. None of them seem to work all that well and the struggle begins.

Is the system helping? If I don't use the system will I succeed? Will the system help me feel the success?

GOAL SETTING

We all know we are supposed to goal set. And the statistics range from 80-90 percent of us never write down a single goal. If we know it is so great for us why don't we?

Personally, I have found that traditional goal setting rarely produces results. It is more like that New Year's resolution that we all make out of obligation with no intent of actually achieving. We are just being part of the crowd—not goal warriors.

Of course, there are other reasons traditional goal setting doesn't work. From analysis paralysis to just no clear way to get from A to B, this ironically doesn't work for the most success driven people around.

"TO-DO LISTS"

"To do" lists are important for keeping your mind focused, but they aren't a goal setting method. Too many of us sit down and say "I want to do X" so to do that I need to accomplish the next 147 tasks.

Being able to organize and understand strategically what needs to happen between here and there is excellent. But when you are faced with just a list of tasks with no clearly defined pay offs, perspectives, and vision- a "to do" list quickly becomes a list of tasks with no purpose or passion behind them and in turn quickly become a list of undone items.

DREAM BOARDS

Their popularity hit their peak awhile back, but they are still out there. Though scarcer than before, the invitations still come to meet up, pay a ridiculous amount in magazines to tear them all apart over a bottle of wine.

Dream boards can have their place, these beautiful masterpieces usually just sit on the wall. No direction, motivation, simply a moment of beauty throughout the day. Though important, it won't accomplish our goals. So, the beauty we see, will be all it will ever be. We'll never walk on the beautiful white sand beaches, drive the Bentley, have that perfect soul stirring romantic relationship without intentional action.

TIME

The biggest culprit for many of us: time. We know we all have 24 hours in a day, yet many days you are left wondering "where did the day go?"

Even if you map out your hours putting in the "must" dos, family, sleep, food, and everything else you must do—you realize that you seriously don't have enough time.

And then one day it hit me. None of this is ever going to work. There is a lot of doing going on, but not a lot of achievement. I needed a way to achieve that allowed my perfectionist ways not to take over, that wasn't hustle obsessed, that wasn't the "build as you go" bullshit, that didn't need 500 steps before I could see results and that made sense.

One day at the gun range with my shooting instructor, the clarity came. Goals are not tangible accomplishments. Those are milestones. Goals are bigger, deeper, intangible greatness and external fulfillment of something internal. Goals are less about a "to do" and more about a SOUL TARGET we are aiming for.

SOUL TARGET gives an easy way for "Type A"'s to stay organized and recognize success no matter if they hit their goal target spot on or not. Here is how to find your SOUL TARGET.

DEFINE THE PERFECT TARGET

If you have multiple targets, repeat this process, and begin to see how they layer on top of each other. And if one target feels too big, break it down.

TARGET #1

WHAT: Write one sentence defining your target. The fewer words the better.

_____

_____

_____

_____

WHEN: Date it.

_____

WHY for you?

_____

_____

_____

_____

_____

WHY for them?

_____

_____

_____

_____

_____

TARGET #2

WHAT: Write one sentence defining your target.
The fewer words the better.

_____

_____

_____

_____

WHEN: Date it.

_____

WHY for you?

_____

_____

_____

_____

_____

_____

WHY for them?

_____

_____

_____

_____

_____

_____

TARGET #3

WHAT: Write one sentence defining your target.
The fewer words the better.

_____

_____

_____

_____

WHEN: Date it.

_____

WHY for you?

_____

_____

_____

_____

_____

WHY for them?

_____

_____

_____

_____

_____

DEFINE YOUR PERSONAL OUTCOME

What is the perfect personal outcome you are looking for?

_____

_____

_____

_____

_____

_____

_____

_____

_____

_____

_____

What is the range from acceptable to awesome you will accept and why?

_____
_____
_____
_____
_____
_____
_____
_____
_____
_____
_____

What does this outcome mean for your personal relationships? Family? Friends? Kids?

_____
_____
_____
_____
_____
_____
_____
_____
_____
_____

DEFINE YOUR PROFESSIONAL OUTCOME

What is the perfect professional outcome you are looking for?

_____
_____
_____
_____
_____
_____
_____
_____
_____
_____
_____
_____

What is the range from acceptable to awesome you will accept and why?

_____
_____
_____
_____
_____
_____
_____
_____
_____
_____

What does this outcome mean for your staff? Business?

_____
_____
_____
_____
_____
_____
_____
_____
_____
_____

Here is how I lay this out visually. Plus, you check out a video at http://soultarget.com.

Now that your SOUL TARGET is defined (step 1) and your personal and professional outcomes are defined, the tasks to get you there become clear. And—all "Type A" people know how to get their "to do" on!

Here is why I love looking at my projects in a SOUL TARGET kind of way. Because rarely will I achieve my goal dead on perfect. My perfectionist ways will notice that I am slightly off and then internally I don't give myself the "win." The SOUL TARGET Method allows me to win as long as I am in the range of acceptable. Sometimes I win a bit more on the personal side or may be a bit more on the business side, but as long as I am in that box. I am good to go. I am achieving. And in the end, it isn't about the sole action it is about achieving the SOUL TARGET.

NOW THAT SUCCESS AND LIFE IS ROOTED IN RELATIONSHIPS WITH MYSELF FIRST AND OTHERS SECOND.

LEARN.

EVERYTHING IN LIFE IS BASED ON RELATIONSHIPS.

DO.

RELATIONSHIPS ARE ABOUT CREATING A SPACE OF
UNCONDITIONAL LOVE. TAKE A MOMENT AND AUDIT THE
RELATIONSHIPS IN YOUR LIFE. DO YOU NEED TO BE
SUPPORTED? ARE YOU SUPPORTING THE OTHER PERSON THE
WAY THEY NEED TO BE SUPPORTED? REVIEW YOUR
RELATIONSHIPS INDIVIDUALLY AND WITH THE OTHER PARTY
WITH THE INTENT OF FULFILLING EVERYONE'S GOALS IN WAYS
THAT MEET THEIR LOVE LANGUAGE AND INNATE HUMAN NEEDS.

BELIEVE.

HAVING OUTSTANDING RELATIONSHIPS IS TOTALLY POSSIBLE
FOR YOU IN EVERY AREA OF YOUR LIFE.

BECOME.

PAUSE AND CONSCIOUSLY FOCUS YOUR INTENTION AND ATTENTION ON THE RELATIONSHIPS THAT MATTER THE MOST TO YOU.

CONNECT.

SET MONTHLY RELATIONSHIP GOALS FOR YOURSELF. IF THAT IS HOW MANY NEW PEOPLE YOU MEET, CONNECTING DEEPER WITH A FRIEND, GOING TO A NETWORKING EVENT AND HAVING THREE COFFEE DATES WITH PEOPLE YOU MEET OR GOING ON A REAL DATE. BY GOING OUT OF YOUR RELATIONSHIP COMFORT ZONE YOU GET TO KNOW YOURSELF BETTER AND LEARN HOW TO USE YOUR NERI TOOLS TO CONNECT WITH OTHERS AUTHENTICALLY AND QUICKER TOO.

BUILDING THE RIGHT BRAND RELATIONSHIP FOR YOU

The simple truth, you control your brand. Yep, from how much you charge, to who you serve, what you do to how you do it - you choose it all. Which also means you choose the brand relationships you have as well.

Now choosing your brand relationships may not sound sexy and you may think, "What is there to choose?" the truth is that defining your brand relationships are essential to have the profitable, fulfilling, and successful brand you want.

And when your brand relationships are on point you can say goodbye to the clients that never convert, the unappreciation, nickel and diming approach, and always wanting massive extras. Yes, your brand relationship when done right-puts all of this in its place.

HERE IS HOW:

Use the following space to define all of the types of brand relationships you have. Yep, everyone is not created equal and nor should the relationship be expected to be.

_____
_____
_____
_____

From your above list, write what you want out of each of the relationships as well as what the brand needs from each of the relationships.

_____
_____
_____
_____
_____
_____
_____
_____

In a third section, write HOW you would enjoy fulfilling your half of the relationship and specifically how you want the other party to react.

_____

_____

_____

_____

_____

_____

_____

Is there a defining moment when the initial relationship is over, i.e. services rendered, if so, what is the cue and how does the relationship transition?

_____

_____

_____

_____

_____

_____

_____

_____

_____

In a different color pen, write what you can do or already do within your brand to create that result?

_____

_____

_____

_____

_____

_____

Once you are clear about the intention of every relationship—what to do, say, implement and act becomes crystal clear. And all of those moments of self-doubt or "should I or shouldn't I" fade away too.

Besides bringing you a lot of personal peace you also create clear roles and expectations for your staff and clients. Helping them see you as the true expert and leader that you are.

I KNOW THAT THE CHOICE TO INFLUENCE IS UP TO ME.

LEARN.

THE IMPRESSIONS YOU MAKE EQUAL THE INFLUENCE AND
INCOME YOU CREATE.

DO.

YOU CAN NEVER CONSCIOUSLY AND STRATEGICALLY MANAGE 50,000+ IMPRESSIONS A DAY EVEN IF YOU HAD THE PERSONAL HANDLERS OF THE KARDASHIANS. THE BEST WAY TO MAKE SURE YOU ARE MAKING THE MOST OUT OF THESE 50,000 DAILY OPPORTUNITIES IS BY ALWAYS SHOWING UP AS THE BEST VERSION OF YOU.

BELIEVE.

SELF + SERVICE = SUCCESS.

BECOME.

BY BEING A PERSON OF INTENTION FIRST AND ACTION SECOND
YOU CREATE AN UNSPOKEN PRESENCE AND DESIRABILITY OF
WHO YOU ARE AND WHAT YOU ARE ABOUT.

CONNECT.

LEARN HOW TO MASTER THE 7 FIGURE SIGNALS, INTELLIGENT INFLUENCE, AND OWNING ANY ROOM IS PART ART AND PART SCIENCE. WE HAVE AN EVER-GROWING LIST OF MINI COURSES ON THESE TOPICS ALL DESIGNED TO GIVE YOU BITE SIZE INFORMATION IN WHICH YOU CAN TAKE ACTION AND SEE RESULTS FAST AVAILABLE AT THE SUCCESS REBEL ACADEMY (HTTP://SUCCESSREBELACADEMY.COM).

ALI'S FAVORITE BVYS

Over the years of serving a unique community, it is natural that I've found some things work better than others. Here, I share my top eight BEST VERSION OF YOU (BVY) hacks.

1. HOW TO OWN YOUR STATUS

Blame it on being a startup or just the simple fact that you don't have a gazillion letters behind your name. It can be a challenge for an entrepreneur to truly own the fact that they truly know their stuff.

The easiest way to overcome such a mindset game (and yes, that is really all it is, a mental game at hand) put facts on your side. Make a list of everything that makes you an expert. It can be formal things like certifications or trainings. And it can be informal elements such as that you have always been damn good at reading people or that constantly redecorating your room as a kid.

All the elements and instances in your life prior to this moment led you up to this exact moment. And you have to believe that on some level you are fully prepared for it on a Divine and down-home level.

2. SAYING "NO"

Often people will say "yes" just because they don't want the perceived confrontation and drama of saying "no." And though it can feel like this is the less painful approach the truth is it isn't for you or for them.

The following are how you say "no" and not feel like an ass.

1. Know your opinion. Half the time we say "yes" because we don't know how we truly feel about the situation, so we say "yes" in the moment and then regret our choice later.

2. Know your boundaries. Know how you feel about situations and how far you are willing to bend with people. Do you hate waking up early, then don't say "yes" to a friend's request to host a 5k race that starts at dawn, Make your boundaries nonnegotiable to you and to everyone else.

3. Know your end goals. Know what you are looking for out of every situation- aka know your intentions. When you know this, you instinctually begin to know when you need to say "no."

And if you ever find yourself in the situation where you have applied the above steps and you still want to say "no." Here is how you do it.

"No. Thank you."

No explanation. No "because." No "I'm sorry." All you need to say is "No. Thank you." and move on.

3. WHEN YOU AREN'T FEELING THE LOVE

In business and in your personal life, it is easy to have moments where you don't feel the love.

Baring that the issue isn't with you- aka you are personally grounded- it can be hard to broach the topic that a relationship isn't living up to what you want it to be.

Use the following ways to make sure that this intimate conversation goes exceptionally well.

1. Location matters. Do a little reconnaissance and choose a neutral location that is new to both you and your client.

2. Timing matters. Neither party should be rushed to arrive or to leave.

3. Inquire about them 85% of the time. You are clearly feeling hurt. But most likely your pain is stemming from their pain. Do NOT jump into "it's all about your conversation" because it isn't. It is all about them.

4. Listen. Not with your ears, but with your heart. Stay focused and grounded in the moment. No matter what they say, no matter if they get accusatory, stay in the moment, and listen openly.

5. Don't stop asking questions or start replying until they have nothing else to say.

6. Repeat. Once they are completely done talking, repeat what you heard, acknowledge it, and then state how you feel- factually, not dramatically.

7. Don't leave until there is a resolution. Even if the resolution is to agree to disagree, it still is a resolution.

What does any of this have to do with how you feel?

Relationships are a two-way street. And most likely if you aren't happy, they aren't happy either. By taking the steps to create a supportive and neutral environment for both of you- true resolution can occur. By allowing the other party to speak first an4fully you allow them to be heard. The simple act of truly hearing someone is the greatest gift and most honoring act you give to someone. This act of respect allows you to have a full picture of what is going on and shows your heart for the relationship.

Plus, by the time you get to the end, your pain doesn't feel so bad anymore.

Perspective is a particularly good thing.

4. HOW TO HANDLE A CRISIS WITH GRACE AND EASE

Let's just cut to the chase. Crisis will come.

If it is to your industry, your life, your business, or your community- to think that the impressions you make will always be drama free and never under attack is a bit foolish.

Like with every other disaster that comes your way, preparation is a girl's best friend.

So, when it comes to prepping your brand and the impressions you make for crisis management, consider these Olivia Pope "exec" techniques.

1. Know where you stand. Know the how's and whys of what you do. Know where you stand against or with the social and industry norms.

2. Know the real enemy. Is it a personal accusation? An industry wide shake down? Of an industry influencer trying to make themselves look better.

3. Choose your mode. If the crisis doesn't have anything to do with you directly take the educational approach. Educate people on why this happened and how it can be fixed.

If it is an accusation directly about you, take the opaque approach instantly. The opaque approach is somewhat transparent, but the details are a bit fuzzy. By being opaque about the situation you can ease concerns, but not allowing people to get caught up on the finer details that don't truly matter. For example, she used a red pen to sign her name. That is a sign she was out for blood. Or it could be that she just liked writing in red ink or that was the only pen around.

Being opaque vs. transparent helps to keep the audience's focus on the resolution and not go down the rabbit hole of details.

Be prepared for when a crisis comes. Create practice scenarios that are business or industry specific that you can run through to keep your mind sharp and your skill ready. Because one day this won't be a drill.

5. HOW TO OWN THE PHONE

Video meetings may be all the rage, but phones are not dead.

And though video meetings do convert better because you get to read a fuller picture of each other's nonverbal communication there are a few things you can do to increase your influence even when you are on the phone.

1. Stand up. The simple act of standing up will have you feeling more confident and sounding more confident.

2. Use a mirror. We naturally mirror other people, even ourselves. So yes, watching yourself talk will increase your energy and enthusiasm.

3. Be handsfree. Allow yourself to be as free flowing with your conversation as if the two of you were in person. Free your hands and let them talk too.

4. Actively hear. Active listening is about hearing the unspoken words, picking up on the tone and vibe. Many times, this leads to the truth about what is really holding them back from saying yes or moving forward.

5. The pause. When you are on the phone, you can't see when the other person has stopped talking. Use this to your advantage. Society has trained us to not like the silence within a conversation so if you make sure to pause between each person talking one of two things will happen. (1) the other person will keep talking giving you a better insight into what is really going on and (2) you come across as owning the conversation because of your cool, calm, and collected way.

Though the telephone may not be in vogue, sometimes it can be your best friend.

6. WHEN TO SIT AND WHEN NOT TO DO SO

In many situations the act of sitting down is a position of weakness, but not always.

Here are two scenarios where taking a seat actually means you keep your influence.

1.   When you feel you are more important than the person greeting you. I know that sounds bad, but it is true. If someone comes to greet you and you are already seated. You stand to meet them as a sign of respect. If you don't feel respect is needed, no need to stand.

2.   When someone wants to talk business. Many times, we feel like we have to be top dog, or should I say "talk dog" to win a business negotiation. And yes, biologically the bigger opponent wins, but not always. If you are already seated, staying seated is "standing" your ground. Also, if you can have the other person "come down to your level" by sitting next you- you actually have the upper hand.

It is in these situations where knowing intention is way more valuable than getting trapped in standard societal protocol.

7. HOW TO NEGOTIATE FROM AUTHENTIC POWER

Have you noticed that everything is a negotiation?

At least people feel that way.

Let's negotiate the price, relationship, deliverables, timeframe, scope- things that make absolutely no sense people feel are negotiable. Some things are simply non-negotiable

Here is how to create the "nonnegotiable" influence without ever having to say it.

1. Stand your ground literally. The simple act of standing gives you your greatest strength and it shows.

2. Keep your voice on an even keel. When we are nervous, we tend to raise our vocal tones and that raised tone at the end of a thought can turn the statement into a question open for discussion.

3. Be head on. No matter if it is a video conferencing or in person, face the other person and the situation head on.

4. Stay open. When we are nervous, we tend to put barriers, a purse, notebook, table between yourself and the other person. Being bare in this situation shows strength and an unapologetic nature. So, remove the barriers.

5. Wear black. Or any dark color for that matter. In Western society, the darker the color the more professional the person or situation is viewed.

If you don't want to negotiate, you don't have to.

8. HOW TO OVERCOME YOUR NERVES

Being nervous happens. Nervous to close the deal, take the stage, meet the future step kids- being nervous is part of life. But you don't have to let your sweaty palms, wobbly knees, and butterfly feeling stomach control you.

The biological responses to being nervous is our fight or flight mode in overdrive. Too much adrenaline flooding our system that it has no idea what to do with it all—and because you aren't running for your life away from a mountain lion—your body rids itself in sweats, shakes, and the occasional pukes. All of these things create obviously poor nonverbal communication skills.

But when you begin to feel the signs of extreme nervousness consider the following solutions:

1. Move. If it is running a marathon or walking across the stage. Just move.

2. Hold your core in. By holding your abdominal muscles in you are allowing yourself to stand up as straight as possible which means you can

breathe, but you also are bringing more blood flow to the area as well.

3.   Pause and be in the moment. Our nervousness comes from us thinking about the future. Stop. Take a breath and enjoy the people and experience at hand.

When you learn what combination works best for controlling your nervousness, you will have your nonverbal communication and influence back on track.

I KNOW THAT THE REAL ME IS THE ONLY VERSION OF ME THAT THIS WORLD NEEDS.

LEARN.

HABITS DON'T HAVE TO KEEP HOLDING YOU BACK. YOU CAN
CHOOSE TO AUTHENTICALLY CHANGE THE HABITS THAT ARE
SABOTAGING YOUR SUCCESS.

DO.

UNDERSTANDING WHO YOU AREN'T ISN'T BEING SELFISH, PRIDEFUL, OR ANY OTHER SOCIAL STORY THE OTHERS WANT TO THROW YOUR WAY. BY UNDERSTANDING YOUR TRUE SELF, YOU CAN BEGIN TO MAKE CHOICES THAT EMPOWER YOUR WORK, RELATIONSHIP, AND LIFESTYLES.

BELIEVE.

NEVER FORGET THAT THE REAL YOU IS REALLY WORTH KNOWING.

BECOME.

BE THE PERSON THAT PEOPLE WANT TO HAVE RELATIONSHIPS
WITH BECAUSE YOU WANT TO HAVE GENUINE, HONEST, NO
ALTERNATIVE MOTIVE RELATIONSHIPS WITH THEM FIRST.

CONNECT.

PERSONALLY, I FIND THAT LEARNING ABOUT NERI IS BEST DONE IN A SMALL GROUP BECAUSE YOU ARE ABLE TO UNDERSTAND YOURSELF AND SEE THE OTHER OPTIONS OF WHO YOU COULD CHOOSE TO BE MODELED IN FRONT OF YOU. I PERSONALLY LEAD TWO NERI SMALL GROUPS A YEAR. YOU CAN GET MORE DETAILS ON THAT AND NERI OVERALL AT (HTTP://NERI.IO).

I NEVER GET IN MY OWN WAY.

LEARN.

WE CAN USE OUR BIOLOGY, SUBCONSCIOUS TRIGGERS, AND
SOCIAL STORIES TO OUR ADVANTAGE.

DO.

BEGIN TO TAKE BACK YOUR CONTROL BY USING YOUR ENERGY, INSTINCT, AND ENVIRONMENTS TO YOUR ADVANTAGE. BEGIN TO TAKE NOTICE OF WHERE AND WHEN YOU THINK CLEARLY, HAVE MORE ENERGY, MORE CREATIVITY, FEEL HAPPIER, MORE IN LOVE, MORE CONNECTED WITH YOURSELF AND OTHERS. THEN TAKE THAT INFORMATION AND BEGIN TO DISCERN "WHY." ONCE YOU KNOW THAT REPEAT, REPEAT, REPEAT.

BELIEVE.

YOU ARE MORE POWERFUL THAN YOU KNOW.

BECOME.

BEGIN TO PLAN THE IMPORTANT STUFF OF LIFE, WORK, AND YOUR **SOULFIRE** AROUND THE PLACES AND TIMES THAT HAVE YOUR PRIMED FOR SUCCESS. MEANING, IF YOU NEED TO HAVE AN IMPORTANT HEART TO HEART CONVERSATION AND YOU ARE CALMER IN THE AFTERNOON TAKING A WALK—SET YOUR CONVERSATION UP FOR SUCCESS BY HAVING IT IN THE AFTERNOON ON A WALK.

CONNECT.

WE HAVE BEEN TAUGHT FROM AN EARLY AGE NOT TO CONNECT WITH OUR BIOLOGICAL AND ENERGETIC SIDES OF OURSELVES. BEGIN TO EXPLORE WHAT WORKS FOR YOU. GO WITH AN INVESTIGATOR MINDSET AND EXPLORE WHAT WORKS FOR YOU— NOT NECESSARILY EVERYONE ELSE.

I FULLY LIVE MY SOUL'S DESIRES.

LEARN.

IT IS YOUR PERSPECTIVE THAT MAKES YOU A SUCCESS OR
SOMEONE WHO SIMPLY SETTLES.

DO.

DON'T FALL FOR THE SOCIAL STORY THAT YOU ARE SO SPECIAL THAT NOTHING BAD WILL EVER HAPPEN TO YOU. ESPECIALLY AS YOU STEP OUT IN A BIG WAY KNOW THAT OPPOSITION WILL COME. AND WHEN IT DOES DON'T LOOK AT IT AS A SETBACK. LOOK AT IT AS PROOF THAT YOU ARE ON THE RIGHT SOULFIRE PATH.

BELIEVE.

OPPOSITION IS NO OBSTACLE.

BECOME.

NEVER FORGET THAT YOU ARE RUNNING YOUR OWN RACE.
DON'T BE THE PERSON WHO GETS LULLED INTO BELIEVING THAT
THE ONLY WAY YOU CAN SUCCEED IS UNDER THE OTHERS'
TERMS AND TIMEFRAMES.

CONNECT.

I CAN'T STOP SAYING IT ENOUGH, FIND A COMMUNITY THAT WORKS FOR YOU, EVEN IF IT IS A COMMUNITY OF TWO. BEING AROUND LIKE MINDED, SUCCESS REBELS IS THE BEST WAY FOR YOU TO SUCCEED ON YOUR TERMS. AND IF THE SUCCESS REBEL SOCIETY ISN'T FOR YOU, REACH OUT TO ME AT (HTTP://ALICRAIG.COM) AND WE WILL SEE WHAT WE CAN DO.

I KNOW HOW TRULY STRONG I AM.

LEARN.

SOCIETY IS EVOLVING AT A FASTER PACE THAN EVER BEFORE. WHERE BRANDS USE TO EVOLVE THEIR LOOK AND MESSAGING EVERY 4-6 YEARS. BRANDS ARE DOING IT EVERY 4-6 MONTHS AND FASTER NOW. THIS MEANS THAT THE SOCIAL STORIES THAT YOU HAVE GROWN UP WITH MAY NOT HAVE THE SAME CONNOTATION OR SOCIAL BIAS AS THEY USE TO.

DO.

SUCCESS REBELS ARE LEADERS AND AS A LEADER YOU NEED TO TAKE PROACTIVE MEASURES IN EVALUATING IF THERE IS A CHANGE IN A SOCIAL STORY THAT MAY AFFECT HOW YOU PRESENT YOURSELF, SOULFIRE, OR LIVE YOUR LIFE OF NEW NOTORIETY. TO THE WORLD.

BELIEVE.

YOUR INFLUENCE AND INTENTION ARE ALWAYS YOUR CHOICE.

BECOME.

BE CONSCIOUS ABOUT THE EBBS AND FLOWS OF YOUR BODY. BEING A POWERFUL SUCCESS REBEL MEANS YOU ARE A WARRIOR. TAKE CARE OF YOURSELF ON ALL LEVELS SO THAT YOU CAN NEVER BE TAKEN ADVANTAGE OF.

CONNECT.

RECOGNIZE HOW THE SHIFTING SOCIAL STORIES CAN BE USED
TO YOUR ADVANTAGE. BY CONNECTING WITH PEOPLE IN
COMPLEMENTARY FIELDS WHERE YOUR AUDIENCE CROSSES
OVER, YOU ARE ABLE TO SEE POTENTIAL SHIFTS IN YOUR WORK
EARLY ON ALLOWING YOU TO BE THE TRUE INFLUENCER EVEN
MORE TO YOUR COMMUNITY.

SOCIETAL STORY SHIFTS

We have been raised with social stories since before we were born. Use the left column below to write the social stories that you see with yourself, within your industry, and with your relationship roles. Then use the right column to write out what society says about those stories today.

Not sure how to do that?

Watch current social media and entertainment to discover the current social story. Then decide if this new perspective is true for you. If it isn't then clarifying your communication and presence is essential.

I KNOW THAT SUCCESS COMES TO THE COMMITTED FEW.

LEARN.

YES, GOING IT ALONE WILL KILL YOU AND YOUR ABILITY TO TRULY LIVE YOUR LIFE OF NEW NOTORIETY. BUT THAT DOES NOT MEAN YOU NEED A GAGGLE OF FOLLOWERS EITHER. EVEN ONE HAVING YOUR BACK AND CHEERING YOU ON IS BETTER THAN NONE. AND HINT, YOU ALREADY HAVE YOUR ONE— YOUR DIVINE PARTNER.

DO.

FIND WAYS THAT CONNECT THAT FEEL GOOD TO YOU.

BELIEVE.

NO ONE OR THING CAN STOP YOU WITH YOUR DIVINE PARTNER
BY YOUR SIDE.

BECOME.

CONSCIOUSLY BREAK OUT OF YOUR SHELL AND SHY HABITUAL WAYS BY USING YOUR UNIQUE NERI PROFILE, BIOLOGY, ENVIRONMENT, ENERGY AND SUBCONSCIOUS MIND TO YOUR ADVANTAGE.

CONNECT.

Don't let The Others fool you that you are alone or so out there that no one can understand. There are so many reasons that connection even on a small level is important for you—even if it is just to have the reassurance that what you think is false—is more powerful than you know.

we believe that

success is our destiny. our life is no accident. we all have a unique Divine purpose—aka a Soulfire
our dreams are road markers on our life's path. we are the hands and feet in a greater Divine partnership.
relationships rooted in yourself first and others second

Soulfire is like art

success comes from service. shedding the mindset of political correctness. people are born knowing love and learning fear. everything can turn around in an instant. energy creates income. you can always choose again. we are all growing into the true depths of our capabilities. if we are on this side of Heaven there is more for us to do.

our intentions rule everything

success doesn't happen solo. consistency is king. it is our duty to show a little more love in everything we do. unseen and seen forces create the influence, grace, and New Notoriety we seek. success requires both heart and love. success doesn't look the same to any two people. our role as leaders is to influence intelligently the people we are called to serve. our personalities, ability, and authentic reactions are greater than our habits. there is a solution to everything. in stepping out into our true calling we make it easier for the ones around us to step out in theirs. we must take care of ourselves before we can serve others.

APPENDIX
RESOURCES

SUCCESS REBEL GO GUIDE.

I have loads of resources I created just for you and this book at http://SuccessRebelBook.com. Here you can grab your free digital copy of *Success Rebel Go Guide*. The Go Guide has many of the exercises I talk about at the end of each chapter ready and waiting for you to go take action.

SUCCESS REBEL SOCIETY.

And because community, connection, and love are so important I highly encourage you to check out the online and real-world community my team and I run at http://successrebelsociety.com. I create a monthly area of focus for our society members to help excel personally and professionally by fully stepping into their badass selves.

From 21-day action plans to access to the mini courses available at the Success Rebel Academy, and of course live office hours as well as meet ups around the world. My team and I strive to create the supportive environment that all Success Rebels need to excel. Use the code "I AM A Success Rebel" to get 10 free days in the society.

PODCAST NIRVANA.

If you love to listen and learn we have you covered. Head on over to Notoriety Network's (http://notorietynetwork.com) and check out all of the podcasts we have in store for you. Now these aren't your average podcasts. As with everything I do, I want to give you the most bank for your investment. Concise, to the point, and action oriented are what these podcasts are.

Pay special attention to the following ones:

- Success Rebel (well, duh!)

- The Human Element (all about Neuro Human Branding)

- Intelligent Influence CEO (all about Intelligent Influence and Impression Management)

- SOULFIRE Life (all about living your SOULFIRE everyday)

- Meet NERI (all about the NERI profile method for yourself and relationships)

LIVING THE SUCCESS REBEL CEO LIFE.

It is one thing to live your SOULFIRE and life of NEW NOTORIETY in your everyday life. But when your Divine partnership leads you into a business, you aren't just upping your Success Rebel game. You are up leveling your vision, visibility, and best version of you at hyper speed.

Our Success Rebel CEO intensive is an in-person training and multimedia platform designed to create social proof about your message, elevate your industry visibility while leveraging your influence with your branding and marketing efforts as well as with national and international media outlets. Learn more about these in person incentives at http://successrebelceo.com

ABOUT THE AUTHOR

Three-time bestselling author and luxury neuro human branding expert, Ali Craig, combines over twenty years of real world, how to, goal achieving success into one book.

Ali Craig shares the real stories, science, and spirituality of how people have broken through the mediocrity of social success to discover their Success Rebel way. By allowing them to live their dreams and eventually living a life of influence, grace, and NEW NOTORIETY. In her latest work, Craig breaks through the social stories and subconscious triggers that she has helped so many of her entrepreneurial clients struggle with over the years as they strive for success on their terms.

A sought-after national media expert in the United States and international speaker, Ali Craig, is the creator of the widely respected NERI profiling method and is the founder of the International Society of Intelligent Influence. Craig also is the founder of Entreventure Productions, Entreventure Events, and the

Notoriety Network projects all designed to empower the modern-day entrepreneur.

Ali Craig splits her time between New York City, Las Vegas, Nevada, and Phoenix, Arizona where she is a kitty mom to eight wildly spoiled cats.

SISTER BRANDS

Hey Beautiful,

Yes, within these pages I talked about a lot of businesses and many of them are mine. Every single company - besides being separate legal entities and governed under their own unique rules and disclaimers (read that as check out each website for all of the legal specifics) - were created out of my SOULFIRE.

For me, my SOULFIRE is all about creating and protecting beauty and love on this side of Heaven.

What is more beautiful, and honoring, than:

Helping a fellow human birth their SOULFIRE and Divine partnership into life?

Helping another human feel connected, understand themselves better, or create relationships that are deep and meaningful in a timely manner.

Discovering that everything that they have been told that is wrong inside of them is perfect, beautiful, and is the exact Divine message needed to transform their lives and the lives of the ones they influence.

Yes, my SOULFIRE has shown up in many variations over the years. But the heart of my heart has always been the same—to create and protect beauty and love.

Today I have a few projects that help me create and protect beauty and love for myself, fellow entrepreneurs, the people we serve, and the world at large through our Success Rebel Society, Success Rebel Academy, NERI, Society of Neuro Human Branding and the International Society of Intelligent Influence. I invite you to explore and see what my Divine partnership has created.

My intention for every engagement with you is that you know that you are loved, know that you are not alone, and are reminded of the Divine that lives inside of you. You can check out all of my sister brands at http://alicraig.com/sisterbrand

www.ingramcontent.com/pod-product-compliance
Lightning Source LLC
Chambersburg PA
CBHW060306030426
42336CB00011B/956